David Humphreys'
"Life of General Washington"
with George Washington's "Remarks"

DAVID HUMPHREYS'

"Life of
General Washington"

with

George Washington's "Remarks"

EDITED, WITH AN INTRODUCTION,
BY ROSEMARIE ZAGARRI

The University of Georgia Press
Athens and London

© 1991 by the University of Georgia Press
Athens, Georgia 30602
All rights reserved

Designed by Sandra Strother Hudson
Set in Janson by Tseng Information Systems
Printed and bound by Thomson-Shore
The paper in this book meets the guidelines
for permanence and durability of the Committee on
Production Guidelines for Book Longevity of
the Council on Library Resources.

Printed in the United States of America

95 94 93 92 91 C 5 4 3 2 1

Library of Congress Cataloging in Publication Data

Humphreys, David, 1752–1818.
[Life of General Washington]
David Humphreys' life of General Washington : with
George Washington's remarks / edited, with an introduction,
by Rosemarie Zagarri.
p.   cm.
Includes bibliographical references and index.
ISBN 0-8203-1293-2
1. Washington, George, 1732–1799.   2. Generals — United States —
Biography.   3. United States. Continental Army — Biography.
I. Washington, George, 1732–1799.   II. Zagarri, Rosemarie, 1957–
III. Title.   IV. Title: Life of General Washington.
E312.H94   1991
973.4′1′092 — dc20
[B]   90-40542
CIP

British Library Cataloging in Publication Data available

*The Resignation of General Washington, at Annapolis, Maryland,
23 December 1783* (1824–28), painting by John Trumbull.
Courtesy of the Yale University Art Gallery, Trumbull Collection.
Humphreys is the full figure standing immediately behind
Washington.

To Jeff

Contents

Illustrations

Illustrations

Acknowledgments

MORE THAN most historical studies, a documentary edition is a collaborative effort. First and foremost, it is a collaboration between the original authors and the editor; but not incidentally, it involves collaboration — or at least cooperation — between the editor and the present-day owners of the manuscripts being edited. In this case, I am grateful to the Rosenbach Museum and Library, the Yale University Library, and the *Forbes Magazine* Collection for permission to publish documents in their collections.

Many individuals have aided my work, in large ways and small. I would like to thank the graduate students of the 1985 and 1986 classes in historical editing at West Virginia University for suggestions regarding the transcription. I especially thank Alex Lubman, who provided thorough and timely research assistance. The edition has profited from the critical scrutiny of several scholars, including W. W. Abbot, Forrest McDonald, Dorothy Twohig, Don Higginbotham, and Leslie Morris. Dorothy Twohig, in particular, made extremely helpful comments, criticisms, and corrections. Christopher Coover of Christie's, New York, kindly allowed me to see Washington's "Remarks" as it awaited auction. My husband, Jefferson Morley, astutely edited the Introduction. Ellen Harris was a model copyeditor.

My greatest debt is to Leslie Morris, curator of books and

manuscripts at the Rosenbach. She not only suggested the project but provided ongoing intellectual and moral support throughout its extended genesis. She helped identify some of Humphreys' more obscure references, made numerous substantive and editorial suggestions, and initiated me into the subtleties of documentary editing. Although Washington may not be pleased to see his remarks in print, I am (and I suspect David Humphreys is) most grateful to Ms. Morris for making the project possible.

Introduction

GEORGE WASHINGTON has been the subject of numerous biographies, some popular, some scholarly—but none were authorized by the man himself. Yet Washington did give permission to Lieutenant Colonel David Humphreys, his friend and confidant, to write an authorized account. Scholars have long assumed that Humphreys either did not complete the study, or that if he did, the work did not survive.[1] As late as 1936, a descendant of Humphreys could find no biography of Washington in the Humphreys papers in his possession.[2] In the 1960s, however, the historian James Thomas Flexner rediscovered a part of the manuscript at the Rosenbach Museum and Library and drew on it for his biography of Washington. Even so, Flexner claimed that the Humphreys biography "never got beyond an incoherent jumble."[3] Humphreys' own biographer calls the work "hardly more than a fragment."[4]

The colonel, however, did write a substantial portion of a Washington biography—one which has survived and which is far more than an "incoherent jumble." Washington himself reviewed and corrected parts of the manuscript for accuracy. Unfortunately, the peculiar provenance of the biography has obscured its full significance. The dispersion of the manuscripts to three separate locations has prevented readers from seeing the project as a whole. The biographical writings are buried in notebooks along with speeches, letters, and book summaries.

Disproportionate attention has been given to the comments Washington made on Humphreys' work, while little analysis has been done of the biography itself.

The present edition seeks to rectify these problems. It attempts to construct the biography that Humphreys intended to write, and to place the work in its full historical and literary context. It draws together for the first time all extant parts of the biography and prints Washington's comments along with the text to which they refer. The study also demonstrates that Humphreys did publish an important part of the manuscript during his lifetime — but, for reasons to be explained, he did so anonymously. This edition, then, offers a unique new perspective on the personal lives and careers of both Colonel David Humphreys and his mentor, General George Washington.

Humphreys and Washington

For David Humphreys, born in Derby, Connecticut, in 1752, the American Revolution offered not only the opportunity to pursue a military career but also the occasion for the exercise of his literary talent, such as it was. After receiving a master of arts degree from Yale in 1774, Humphreys became a schoolmaster in Wethersfield, Connecticut, for two years. When the war offered a broader field for his ambitions, he volunteered in 1776 as an adjutant with the Second Connecticut Militia Regiment. He quickly made his way up the military hierarchy, becoming a brigade major at age twenty-five and a lieutenant colonel at twenty-eight. More important, however, were the positions of trust that he soon occupied. Only two years after enlisting, he became aide-de-camp to General Israel Putnam, one of Washington's four major generals. In May 1780, after Putnam suffered a severe stroke, Humphreys was appointed

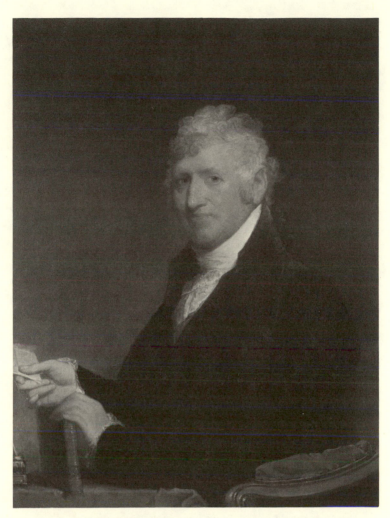

General David Humphreys, painting by Gilbert Stuart. Courtesy of the Yale University Art Gallery, Gift of the widow of General Humphreys in 1830.

aide-de-camp to General Nathanael Greene. No sooner had
he joined Greene than he was appointed aide-de-camp to the
commander-in-chief, General George Washington.[5]

Humphreys' appointments did not come about by chance.
During lulls in the fighting, he had begun to express his sentiments about the war and his country in verse. In the winter of
1779–80 he wrote a poem called "An Address to the Armies,"
in which he praised the American cause and glorified its military heroes. Even before it was published, Humphreys sent a
copy to General Greene, who soon requested Humphreys' re-
assignment to his command. Not long after joining Greene's
staff, Humphreys received the printed version and sent it to
Washington.[6] In one of its more subdued passages, the poem
described Washington in these terms:

> His voice inspir'd, his godlike presence led.
> The Britons saw, and from his presence fled.[7]

Shortly after receiving the poem, Humphreys was transferred
to Washington's command. The literary critic Leon Howard
comments, "Though Washington would never have confused
literary and military ability and Humphreys, of course, had
excellent recommendations as an officer, there is some significance in the fact that the poet was offered the position of
aide-de-camp to the General exactly a month after he had sent
him this token of his genius."[8] Like Greene, Washington may
have wanted a Boswell at his side.

In any case, the relationship between Humphreys and Washington grew into something far more significant than the
young and opportunistic Humphreys may have anticipated. At
this time, a general's aide was considered part of his "military family" and often became the general's confidant as well
as his official assistant. Of course, not all of the thirty-two
aides that Washington had at various times throughout the war

gained his full friendship and trust. But Humphreys was one of those who did. After Yorktown, for example, Washington gave Humphreys the distinction of turning over to Congress the captured British standards. When the war ended, Washington wrote Congress requesting a diplomatic appointment for Humphreys. After Humphreys' return from Europe, Washington invited the colonel to live as part of his family at Mount Vernon. When Washington became president of the United States, he asked his former aide to prepare the first draft of his inaugural address—a speech which, for unknown reasons, Washington chose not to use.[9]

Perhaps because Washington never had any children of his own, he developed closer ties than usual with his aides. After the war, Washington maintained warm relations with many of them, especially Alexander Hamilton, Tench Tilghman, and Judge Robert Hanson Harrison. Without making invidious comparisons in his affection for them, it still seems obvious that Washington considered Humphreys one of his favorites. He became known, according to poet John Trumbull, as the "belov'd of Washington."[10] Who, then, could be better qualified to write the life of General Washington than David Humphreys? Humphreys himself was conscious of his enviable position. He knew, as he said in the Washington biography, that he "possess[ed] an uncommon share in [Washington's] confidence &, in many instances, a full knowledge of his motives, together with a promise from him of whatever manuscript or oral communications were necessary."[11] Although such a biography would have its flaws and biases, it would be a portrait few others could draw.

The Origins and Writing
of the Washington Biography

Humphreys approached Washington about the project as early as 1784, while he was still in Paris as the secretary to a U.S. delegation negotiating commercial treaties. In a letter dated September 30, 1784, Humphreys expounded on the desirability of "some writer [to] assume the pen, who is capable of placing your actions in the true point of light in which posterity ought to view them." [12] He insisted that Washington himself would be best suited for the job, but then proceeded in a not-too-subtle way to promote himself by suggesting a plan for the work. He proposed "arranging the various Events into Campaigns, or 'particular Epochs'" and selecting from Washington's "Letters and Documents everything that is most interesting concerning these events, either by extracting the substance or inserting the whole of such Paper as tended most to elucidate the subject." [13]

Receiving no reply, and aware of Washington's reticence about writing about his own life, Humphreys put himself forward more explicitly for the task. In a January 15, 1785, letter to Washington, Humphreys repeated his views on the need for "a good history of the Revolution, or at least of those scenes in which you have been principally concerned." But he added, "If however you should decline the task, & if ever I shall have leisure and opportunity, I shall be strongly tempted to enter on it, more with the design of rescuing the materials from improper hands or from Oblivion, than from an idea of being able to execute it in the manner it ought to be done." [14] Six months later he still had received no reply. Further emboldened, he wrote, "Since my arrival in France, I have become acquainted with a circle of noble & literary Characters who are passionate admirers of your glory; and since my last letter to you I have been strongly urged by some of them to undertake to write either your life at large, or if I had not leisure and materials for that work, at least a sketch of your life & character." [15]

Humphreys' persistence finally met with success. In late July, Washington gave his enthusiastic approval. The general not only offered to make his private papers available to Humphreys but also suggested that his former aide live at Mount Vernon while working on the project. "I should be pleased indeed," Washington wrote, "to see you undertake this business; your abilities as a writer; your discernment respecting the principles which lead to the decision by arms; your personal knowledge of many facts as they occurred in the progress of the War; your disposition to justice, candour & impartiality, & your diligence in investigating truth, all combining, fit you, when joined with the vigor of life, for this task." [16]

Returning from Europe in 1786, he soon visited Washington. Arriving at Mount Vernon in late July, he set to work on the biography of his mentor. But in a letter to his brother dated August 4, he voiced a curious ambivalence about the project. In part, he seemed daunted by the task. "Here is a noble work before me," he wrote, "but deterred by the magnitude of the enterprise I have not yet had spirit to resolve upon its execution." [17] Nevertheless, he enjoyed his favored position in Washington's eyes. "It affords me no unpleasant reflection," he said in the same letter, "to be convinced that the man in the United States who entertains the most favourable sentiments of my morals and abilities is precisely the greatest man in them." [18] After six weeks with the Washingtons, Humphreys departed for Connecticut.

On his return home, Humphreys was elected to serve in the Connecticut assembly. Throughout the tumultuous autumn of 1786, Humphreys corresponded with Washington and kept him informed about Shays' Rebellion in nearby Massachusetts. Curiously, neither Washington nor Humphreys mentioned the progress of the Washington biography in their letters.[19] At the time, however, Humphreys coauthored, with the "Connecticut Wits," a biting satire on the weaknesses of the confederation called "The Anarchiad: A Poem on the Restoration of Chaos and Substantial Night."[20] On May 13, 1787, Washington and Humphreys met in Chester, Pennsylvania. Each was on his way to a meeting in Philadelphia: Humphreys to a meeting of the Society of the Cincinnati and Washington to the federal constitutional convention.[21]

Shortly thereafter, Humphreys grappled with personal tragedy. He buried both his mother and his father in quick succession, and found himself with few remaining ties to Connecticut. In late September 1787 he wrote to Washington about his situation. Having received a standing invitation to return to Mount Vernon, he asked whether he might now come. Washington responded generously, commenting, "The only stipulations I shall contend for are, that in all things you shall do as you please."[22] After his arrival in early to mid-November, Humphreys became a permanent member of Washington's domestic circle at Mount Vernon, staying there until the general assumed the presidency.[23]

During his long residence at Mount Vernon, Humphreys pursued a number of literary projects. He wrote various poems, translated a French play, *The Widow of Malabar*, into English, and composed his "Essay on the Life of the Honourable Major-General Israel Putnam."[24] Humphreys presented the Putnam biography to a meeting of the Connecticut Society of the Cincinnati on July 4, 1788. When it was published, it became his most enduring popular success.

During his stay Humphreys also wrote the most polished part of the Washington biography, which covers the period from Washington's birth to his retirement after the war. Humphreys began the project during his 1786 visit to Mount Vernon and continued with it while living in Connecticut. After returning to Mount Vernon in 1787, but well before Washington's election to the presidency, he finished it. This section was published without attribution to Humphreys in 1789 as part of Jedidiah Morse's *American Geography*.[25]

Humphreys composed his work in light of Washington's achievements as a general, not with an eye toward Washington the future president. All of the extant outlines for the project, for example, end at or with Washington's retirement to Mount Vernon.[26] Humphreys' preface to the biography stressed that he was presenting a "portrait of the person, who commanded the troops of the Union during the whole term of that perilous struggle, & who afterwards assisted in securing the fruits of the revolution."[27] He concluded his discussion of Mount Vernon by saying, "Such are the philosophic shades, to which the late Commander in Chief of the American armies has retired, from the tumultuous scenes of a busy world."[28] The emphasis was on Washington's successes during the Revolution and his contentedness in retirement, giving a sense of a career that had been finished, rather than one that was about to enter a whole new phase.

After publication Humphreys continued to update the manuscript and add new sections that took account of changes in Washington's life. To the opening discussion of Washington's birth, Humphreys inserted the phrase, "& the first President of the United States under the reformed Constitution."[29] Humphreys observed that Washington abandoned his passion for his favorite sport, foxhunting, and now "went not once to the chace."[30] As the ratification process proceeded, Humphreys wrote new material describing the general's reaction to ratification, his agonizing over the presidency, and his preparations for the new government.

But when did Humphreys write the new material? While it is

impossible to prove definitively, the text offers some clues. The tone and language suggest that he wrote this portion of the manuscript after Washington's election to the presidency but before leaving Mount Vernon for New York; that is, between fall 1788 and April 1789. Unlike any other part of the manuscript, the section contains direct quotes and paraphrases of private conversations between Washington and Humphreys.[31] Although it is possible that the colonel transcribed the conversations immediately after having them, internal evidence suggests he did not. In at least one instance Humphreys misdated by about a month a trip taken by Washington in the summer of 1788 — and hence misdated the conversation that followed.[32] It is unlikely, then, that Humphreys kept an ongoing record of his discussions with Washington. Yet the colonel surely recorded the conversations soon enough after the fact to feel confident that he was portraying them accurately. Although Washington was not officially notified of his election until April 14, 1789, he and Humphreys had received the results of balloting for the presidential electors by the late autumn of 1788.[33] Once Humphreys knew Washington had been elected and was certain that the general would accept the office, he probably decided to memorialize the crucial conversations in which he supposedly persuaded his friend to become the first president. It is, of course, possible that Humphreys wrote these sections much later. But by then the numerous duties of his positions — first as Washington's secretary, then as a diplomat — would have taken precedence over his own writing. Moreover, Humphreys would not have been so certain of the precise wording of the conversations. While the dating thus remains somewhat speculative, it seems likely that Humphreys composed the new material during late 1788 or early 1789.

Provenance of the Manuscripts

The convoluted provenance of the manuscripts containing Humphreys' biography of George Washington reveals some of the problems involved in reconstructing the text. At present, the biography consists of three separate parts in three different locations. One section, at the Rosenbach Museum and Library in Philadelphia, consists of two gatherings, in which the pages have been stitched together as notebooks, and one loose page with writing on both sides. A second manuscript, consisting of forty-four loose pages with writing on only one side of the page, is in the Humphreys-Marvin-Olmsted Collection at Yale University. A third manuscript, in the *Forbes Magazine* Collection in New York City, consists of eleven pages in Washington's handwriting, keyed to volume 2 of the Rosenbach manuscript.

It is unclear how a single work was split into so many parts. It seems that at a very early stage, Washington's "Remarks" was separated from the main body of Humphreys' biography and preserved separately. Humphreys died in 1818, with no children surviving him. His wife, Ann Frances Bulkeley Humphreys, decided in 1829 to give Washington's "Remarks" to a close family friend, John Pickering. Pickering was the son of Colonel Timothy Pickering, who had served with Humphreys in the diplomatic service at Lisbon.[34] A cover sheet accompanying the manuscript is inscribed "Washington—Paper—given to me by Mrs. Humphreys—1829—containing original memoir in Washington's handwriting, by way of remarks upon an intended biography which General Humphreys was writing. [*Signed*] John Pickering."[35] Over the next century the manuscript descended through the Pickering family. In 1936 John Pickering (the younger) of Salem, Massachusetts identified himself as the manuscript's owner in a note published

George Washington's "Remarks," manuscript, page 1.
Courtesy of Christie's, New York, and the *Forbes Magazine*
Collection.

in the *Essex Institute Historical Collections*. John C. Fitzpatrick cited the same Pickering as owner when he published Washington's comments in 1939. However, at some point ownership of the document reverted to the Pickering Foundation in Boston, from whom John F. Fleming, a former employee of the Rosenbach Library, purchased the manuscript in 1974. Malcolm Forbes obtained the document at auction in 1988.[36]

Ironically, it is much easier to trace the descent of Washington's comments on the biography than it is to trace the biography itself. There are no clear records indicating how Humphreys' manuscripts arrived at their respective destinations in the Rosenbach and Yale libraries. Because Humphreys had no children, his papers went to other, less closely related family members and friends. The manuscript at Yale seems to have descended through one branch of the Humphreys family. A genealogy attached to the collection guide provides tantalizing clues about the manuscript's journey over time. Humphreys' brother, John (1744–1832), had a daughter, Anna (1781–1875), who married Elihu Marvin. Their daughter, Sarah (1820–43), married Lemuel Gregory Olmsted. Their daughter, Sarah Lucy (1840–70), married the Honorable Matthew Griswold. Their son, Matthew Griswold (1866–1929), had a son, also named Matthew, born in 1896. This man, who became a doctor, donated the papers to Yale in two parts, in 1957 and 1977.[37]

The origins of the manuscript at the Rosenbach Library are even more obscure. Unlike Washington's "Remarks," the Rosenbach manuscript did not descend through the Pickering family, nor was it in the possession of the Reverend Frank Landon Humphreys of New Canaan, Connecticut, who owned yet another portion of Humphreys' papers.[38] The papers may have been passed down through the Marvin and Olmsted families, as the Yale manuscript was, but disposed of separately. According to Leslie A. Morris, curator of books and manuscripts at the Rosenbach Library, Dr. F. S. W. Rosenbach made a payment in 1935 for $2,250.00 to a Miss Griswold for unspecified "American Documents." [39] This suggests that Dr. Rosenbach may have acquired his manuscript from the same ultimate source as Yale—from the Griswold family—but at an earlier date.

There is no question that the three manuscripts together constitute a single whole. The Forbes manuscript consists of Washington's annotations of the Rosenbach manuscript. Washington, for example, corrected Humphreys' claim that his father had wished him to join the British navy, when, in fact, it was his brother's idea. [40] He noted with pride that Indians during the French and Indian War had named him "Caunotaucarius (in English) the Town-taker." [41] He obligingly filled in information that Humphreys did not know, such as the number of bushels of wheat produced on Washington's farms and the events surrounding his participation in the French and Indian War. [42] Although the Yale manuscript is far more fragmentary and less polished than the manuscript at the Rosenbach, the two are integrally related. Sections of the two documents are nearly identical, such as the discussion of Mrs. Washington's objections to George's joining the British navy or Washington's decision to resign from military service in 1759. [43] Humphreys' discussion of a cabinet for the new government—literally referring to a bureau in which to keep state papers—begins on a loose page in the Rosenbach Collection and continues on a page in the Yale manuscript. [44] There is also much new material in the Yale manuscript which fills in gaps in the earlier narrative or continues the story from the time of the French and Indian War to Washington's assumption of the presidency.

The Humphreys-Marvin-Olmsted Collection also contains a notebook, which holds copies of various documents. One eight-page section consists of an essay apparently intended as an epilogue to Humphreys' "Poem on the Death of General Washington."[45] Humphreys first delivered the poem publicly on July 4, 1800, at the American Legation in Madrid, with the remarks being presented afterward. Although the poem was published several years later, the epilogue never was. I have included it here as part of the "Life of General Washington" because it forms a fitting conclusion to Humphreys' otherwise unfinished work.

Publication History

It has generally been assumed that David Humphreys never published his "Life of General Washington." It is now clear, however, that he did publish a part of it — albeit anonymously — in Jedidiah Morse's 1789 volume, *The American Geography; or, A View of the Present Situation in the United States of America.* Printed in the "Notes" section, the essay ran for five pages, along with sketches of two other Revolutionary War generals, Richard Montgomery and Nathanael Greene. It was subsequently reprinted several times during Humphreys' lifetime, though never attributed to him, in publications such as the *Massachusetts Magazine* of May 1789, in anonymous pamphlets published in 1790 and 1794, and in London in 1792 as an appendix to an oration by Elhanan Winchester.[46]

There is no doubt that Humphreys wrote the sketch published in Morse's geography. The published biography incorporated volume 2 of the Rosenbach manuscript, a single paragraph from the Yale manuscript, and Washington's "Remarks" on Humphreys' work.[47] Long sections of both versions were the same word for word. Both texts discussed, for example, Washington's "inveterate pulmonary complaint"; his daily "rotine"; his attempt to "extricate his troops from the fatal ambuscade into which his [Braddock's] overweening confidence had conducted them," as well as Washington's being "the focus," after his retirement, "of political Intelligence for the New World."[48]

Minor differences between the printed version and Humphreys' handwritten draft were probably made in the process of editing the piece for publication. These changes fall into several categories. First, there were some minor alterations in phrasing, punctuation, paragraphing, and capitalization. These changes were insubstantial and did not alter Humphreys' meaning in any way. One example will suffice to give a flavor of the changes. Humphreys discussed the report that Washington wrote after his first trip to Fort Duquesne. The original manuscript read: "His Journal of proceedings, & official Report to Governor Dinwiddie, which were published, announced to the world that correctness of mind, manliness in style and accuracy in the mode of doing business, which have since rendered him so illustrious in more arduous affairs." Morse's published version, in which I have italicized all differences, read: "His *journal, and report* to *governor* Dinwiddie, which were published, announced to the world that correctness of mind, manliness in style and accuracy in the mode of doing business, which have since *characterised* him in *the conduct of* more arduous affairs."[49]

Second, the printed version incorporated many of Washington's corrections and revisions without comment. For example, Morse's published text noted that Washington's brother Lawrence was appointed adjutant general after (not before) his trip to Cartagena, as Washington commented in one of his notes.[50] Washington's estimates on the agricultural output of Mount Vernon were included. The farm, it said, produced seven thousand bushels of wheat and ten thousand bushels of corn.[51] These changes put Washington's notes to the use that they were intended.

Finally, there were at least four cases in which Morse's published version significantly altered, or added to, the handwritten manuscript. Three of these cases were rather short, involving only a few phrases or sentences.[52] The fourth and most important case concerned the discussion of Fort Necessity. The published version added a whole new paragraph not contained in the handwritten draft. In the original manuscript, Humphreys had included only a few incomplete sentences on the subject, and made a plea for Washington to provide the missing information.[53] Washington composed a nine-page account, which Humphreys apparently condensed and used in the published text.[54] This section represents the only major change from the handwritten version to the published version.

The larger question, however, is this: Why did Humphreys not publish the piece under his own name; or to put it another way, why did he allow Jedidiah Morse to publish it as part of the *American Geography*? Although we have no direct evidence to answer this question, circumstantial evidence provides some clues. It is clear that Humphreys and Morse were personally acquainted. In November 1786 Humphreys wrote a letter of introduction to Washington for Morse, who was traveling throughout the Union to gather information for his geography.[55] Humphreys had, by this time, begun his biography of Washington and may have discussed his work with Morse. Humphreys was certainly aware of the nature of Morse's project.

As time passed, Humphreys may have lost interest in a full-scale biography of Washington. Originally, he had wanted to make extensive use of Washington's papers and to write an exhaustive account of his subject. The surviving outlines suggest how detailed Humphreys hoped to make his account. As he began, however, he seems to have been overwhelmed by the magnitude of the project.[56] Although he did proceed, he may have scaled down his expectations. He noted that he was "determined to write" not just for "the information of posterity" but "for his own amusement."[57] A magnum opus may not have seemed too amusing once he actually tried to write it. Rather than produce the definitive biography of Washington, including original documents, Humphreys may have decided to compose a thumbnail sketch that could be completed quickly and easily.

Furthermore, once Humphreys heard speculation about Washington's becoming president, he may have reconsidered the wisdom of the original project. He may have sensed that any biography would be incomplete, if not premature. Humphreys also probably expected to receive an official position in the new administration. He may have thought it unseemly or improper to publish under his own name a highly flattering portrait of his boss. Or more to the point, he may have feared that Washington, with his strict sense of propriety, would disapprove of such a work.

Under these circumstances, then, it seems plausible that Humphreys could have offered his work to Morse, or agreed to give it to him when asked. As Humphreys well knew, eighteenth-century geographies contained much more than information about a country's physical characteristics. They also included sections on political history, biography, and cultural norms. Morse himself knew that one individual could never produce such a work. In a letter written in 1788 to Jeremy Belknap, Morse commented, "The nature of the work does not admit of much originality. The book must derive merit—if it have any—from the accuracy and good judgment with which it is *compiled*, rather than the genius with which it is *composed*. To save me from the odious character of Plagiarist, general credit will be given in the preface for all selections inserted in the work. To particularize such would be needless and endless."[58]

In the preface to the geography, Morse did acknowledge his dependence on others, noting that he "frequently used the words as well as the ideas of the writers, although the reader has not been particularly apprized of it."[59]

If, then, Humphreys agreed to contribute a sketch on Washington, Morse would have had no reservations about incorporating the work without attribution. Moreover, since the two men remained friends after the geography's publication, it is unlikely that Morse used Humphreys' work without his permission. Although Humphreys did not get credit for the study, he may have been satisfied to see his work in print. As the new government went into operation, Humphreys may have realized that a whole new array of other opportunities awaited him.

Humphreys' biography of Washington has never been published in its entirety. Although some of the Rosenbach manuscript was printed in Humphreys' day, most of the Yale manuscript has never been published. Since Humphreys' time, the *only* part of the biography to be reprinted has been Washington's "Remarks." In May 1893 *Scribner's Magazine* published a section of the "Remarks" dealing with the attack on Braddock's troops. John Pickering allowed the whole document to be transcribed in the January 1936 issue of the *Essex Institute Historical Collections*. John C. Fitzpatrick's monumental collection of Washington's writings also included the general's comments.[60] The repeated publication of the "Remarks," however, only highlights the neglect that has befallen Humphreys' biography, on which Washington's comments were based.

Literary Significance

For all his literary pretensions, Humphreys' literary reputation has not flourished over the years. During his lifetime the colonel published over thirty poems and was considered a major American poet.[61] Recent critics, however, have called his work superficial, wooden, and pompous — even beneath the quality of the other minor early American writers.[62] *The Dictionary of American Biography* rendered one of the harshest judgments, saying that "most of Humphreys' poetry is worthless." [63] Humphreys' biographer put the matter more delicately, asserting that Humphreys wrote "epideictic poetry, a highly stylized form adapted from classical rhetoric and elocution." [64] Humphreys' descendant and biographer, Frank L. Humphreys, was even kinder, saying that "it would be presumptuous to claim for David Humphreys the first place among the poets of the Revolution, although he was more widely read than the others." [65] It is significant that a major recent study of early American writers barely bothers to mention the career of David Humphreys.[66]

Humphreys' most popular prose work, "An Essay on the Life of the Honourable Major-General Israel Putnam," first published in 1788, has also suffered from critical abuse. As early as 1843, John Fellows penned a critique called *The Veil Removed from David Humphreys' "Life of Putnam."*[67] Like Fellows, modern critics fault Humphreys for his "uncritical admiration" of Putnam, which led to numerous distortions and embellishments. One of the most blatant exaggerations involved Putnam's volunteering for service in the Revolutionary War. Humphreys portrayed Putnam as a latter-day Cincinnatus, who literally dropped his plow and rushed off to join the cause, without even changing his clothes.[68] According to Leon Howard, "Humphreys, to the detriment of his character as an accurate biographer, contributed more than any of his associates to the creation of an American patriotic mythology." [69] Currently the work is more highly regarded for its role in the development of American romantic fiction than for its elucidation of Putnam's life.

Given the critical hostility to Humphreys, the resurrection of "The Life of General Washington" only improves its author's literary reputation. Humphreys' prose in the biography is less grandiose and less pretentious than his poetry. In fact, Humphreys wrote at least three poems about Washington, none of which is as elegant or economical as his prose on Washington.[70] Humphreys was capable of converting even the simplest sentiment into an obnoxious verse. In his "Poem on the Death of General Washington" (1800), for example, Humphreys described in saccharine terms Washington's life after his resignation from the French and Indian War:

> In rural cares he plac'd his chief delight,
> By day his pleasure and his dream by night—
> How sweetly smil'd his eye to view his farms,
> In produce rich, display unnumber'd charms;
> While joys domestic sweeten'd every toil,
> And his fond partner paid him smile for smile![71]

In "The Life of General Washington," however, he simply stated: "His health was gradually restored; he married Mrs Custis, a handsome & amiable young widow possessed of an ample jointure; and settled himself as a planter & farmer on the estate where he now resides in Fairfax County. . . . His judgment in the quality of soils, his command of money to avail himself of purchases, and his employment in early life as a Surveyor, gave him opportunities of making advantageous locations, many of which are much improved."[72] This is not to say that no passages in the biography are overwritten. The introduction and the description of Washington's being given command of the Continental Army are particularly grandiose. For the most part, however, Humphreys' prose avoids the worst excesses of his poetry.

Beyond that, Humphreys' "Life of Washington" is far superior to his "Life of Israel Putnam." According to literary

View of Mount Vernon, the Seat of General Washington (1798), engraving by J. Weld. Courtesy of the Library of Congress.

conventions of the time, biographies were supposed to portray public figures as models of civic virtue. Humphreys noted that the Putnam biography would be worthwhile if it "create[d] an emulation to copy [Putnam's] domestic, manly and heroic virtues." [73] His "Life of Washington," he said, would be a success if Washington's "examples of private morality will forever be cited by parents for the imitation of their sons." [74]

In spite of this goal, Humphreys' biography of Washington was relatively free of distortion, exaggeration, or outright falsehood. Humphreys did omit a discussion of sensitive matters, such as Washington's dealings in land speculation, his miscalculations during the French and Indian War, and his ownership of black slaves. He delicately referred to Washington's chronic bowel problem as a "pulmonary complaint." [75] The closest he came to criticizing his mentor was to repeat a statement made by Washington's subordinates during the Revolutionary War: that Washington "sometimes exposed his own person too much, especially in reconnoitring the enemy. In some instances, it would not have been difficult to have killed or taken him prisoner." [76] Such a criticism was, of course, also a testament to the general's bravery. Nevertheless, the core of the biography, while generally approving of Washington, presented his actions in a straightforward narrative style with relatively few authorial interjections. Humphreys did not make up stories to heighten his subject's stature. Perhaps because he realized that Washington might review what he wrote, perhaps because he believed Washington's actions spoke for themselves, Humphreys wrote a text that corresponded well with the known facts and existing accounts of his subject's life. The epilogue, written after Washington's death, was more fulsome than the central sections, yet it too was highly accurate.

Humphreys' literary career did not end with the writing of "The Life of General Washington." Despite a self-proclaimed difficulty in finding the "leisure for belles lettres," Humphreys managed to continue his literary pursuits during his time in Europe as a diplomat.[77] After leaving his position in 1790 as Washington's private secretary, he served in several capacities abroad. He completed a secret mission in Spain and Portugal, followed by a term as the minister resident to the court at Lisbon. In 1793 Washington authorized Humphreys to negotiate with the dey of Algiers to obtain the release of the Algerine captives. In 1796 he became the first full minister plenipotentiary to Spain.[78] During this period he wrote various poems, including "A Poem on Industry," "A Poem on the Love of Country," and "A Poem on the Death of General Washington."[79]

But Humphreys' literary career did end abruptly, at the same time as his diplomatic career. In April 1801 the new president, Thomas Jefferson, recalled Humphreys from his post in Spain. The primary reason for the recall seems to have been partisan: Jefferson was a Democratic-Republican and Humphreys was a high Federalist. Still, the snub seems to have come as a shock to Humphreys. After the war he and Jefferson had served together in Paris and intermittently maintained a polite correspondence.[80] He had assumed Jefferson retained some affection for him. He was mistaken. Reeling with disappointment, Humphreys and his wife, Ann, returned to the United States and settled in Boston. Turning from diplomacy to agriculture, he began to import and raise a superior brand of sheep — Merinos — from Spain. He invested in the Humphreysville Manufacturing Company, whose main purpose was to mill fine woolen cloth, but did little new writing. He oversaw the publication in 1804 of his *Miscellaneous Works* and in 1815 produced his final literary work, a play called "The Yankey in England." Three years later, he died at age sixty-five.[81]

Humphreys' abandonment of literature seems to have been connected with his failure as a diplomat. In both arenas he felt alone and misjudged. He believed his fellow countrymen did not understand the true value of his contributions. During his first diplomatic mission in Paris, he had been celebrated as an American literary figure of note.[82] After his return to the United States, however, he was disappointed to discover that Americans did not have a similar regard for him. "Indeed I have found, by recent experience, as well as by former traveling, a great deal in the world, that a Poet like a Prophet is not without honour except *in his own country*," Humphreys wrote to his brother in 1786.[83] The feelings of resentment seem to have grown over time. In 1806 Jedidiah Morse suggested that Humphreys write a review of John Marshall's new biography of Washington. Despite his obvious qualifications for the task, Humphreys refused. In a letter to Morse dated May 17, 1806, Humphreys spoke of his "disgust at the State of things in America, and my reluctance in writing for the public (particularly, in this country)." Filled with self-pity, he continued, "The Publick has no claim to my literary Services. . . . I prefer the bleating of my Merinos, with which I am surrounded, to all the plaudits that could be lavished by creatures, of less innocent and interested Species. The Revolution of my wheels, from wh[ich] I am confident only good will result, shall superside, in no small degree, my attention to the Revolution of States, whose destinies are to my mind's eye, invelloped in more obscurity."[84] By 1800 Humphreys found the United States an unfamiliar and hostile place—a world in which party divisions dwarfed personal loyalties and cultural ignorance prevented poets from receiving their deserved accolades. Humphreys' decade abroad had made him lose touch with the homeland whose virtues he celebrated so extravagantly in verse.

Washington's Autobiographical "Remarks"

Washington's comments on Humphreys' biography are at least as revealing as the biography itself. At Humphreys' behest the general apparently reviewed the part of the manuscript dealing with his birth up to his retirement at Mount Vernon. Although the bulk of the comments—nine of eleven handwritten pages—dealt with his experiences during the French and Indian War, there were shorter remarks on other aspects of his life. Though written in the third person, the comments represent Washington's reflections on his early life—the closest he ever came to writing his autobiography.

The manuscript exists today only because Humphreys ignored his mentor's wishes. Humphreys had asked for the general's comments, assuring him that "the Original Manuscript shall be either destroyed or restored to the General."[85] At the end of his remarks, Washington picked up the point and "earnestly requested, that after Colonel Humphreys has extracted what he shall judge necessary, and given it in his own language, that the *whole* of what Is here contained may be returned to George Washington, or committed to the flames."[86] Washington did not intend for his words to survive. Yet they do. Because of their private nature, the comments reveal a Washington who is unusually candid and forthright. It is true, as W. W. Abbot points out, that Washington never let down his guard completely, that he was a man who was always "constructing himself" with an eye toward his public image.[87] Nevertheless, his statements to Humphreys reveal a side of Washington that does not often appear in his other writings.

Washington, for example, openly criticized the British and pointed out his own superior judgment during the French and Indian War. In regard to the surprise ambush of Braddock's troops, he noted that "the folly & consequence of op-

Washington in 1772 (1830), engraving by J. W. Steel. Courtesy
of the Library of Congress.

posing compact bodies to the sparse manner of Indian fighting in woods, which had in a manner been predicted, was now so clearly verified that from hence forward another mode obtained in all future operations."[88] He mentioned a fruitless mission to Williamsburg to request more British support for the Virginia troops. Because the aid was not forthcoming, "as George Washington foresaw, so it happened, the frontiers were continually harrassed—but not having force enough to carry the War to the gates of Du Quesne, he could do no more than distribute the Troops along the Frontiers in stockaded Forts."[89] He derided a plan to make all officers with a commission from the Crown superior to those with colonial appointments. This scheme, he said, "was too degrading for George Washington to submit to; accordingly, he resigned his Military employment."[90] He also directed Humphreys to notice his less well known accomplishments. In a footnote discussing his command of the troops during the Revolutionary War, Washington added, "Whether it be necessary to mention that my time & Services were given to the public without compensation, and that every direct and indirect attempt afterwards, to reward them [was refused] . . . you can best judge."[91] Washington, however, clearly felt the need to mention his sacrifice.

Washington was often quite generous in his comments about his fellow officers, both British and American. Although he despised the system which allowed Captain James McKay, an American with a commission from the Crown, to outrank him, a colonel appointed by the governor of Virginia, he nevertheless called McKay "a brave & worthy Officer."[92] General John Forbes, whose plan for taking Duquesne he had bitterly opposed, Washington labeled "a brave & good Officer."[93] Washington even had words of praise for the hapless General Edward Braddock, whose inability to adjust to American conditions resulted in a devastating defeat for his troops. Braddock was a man, he said, "whose good & bad qualities were intimately blended. He was brave even to a fault and in regular service would have done honor to his profession. — His attachments were warm — his enmities strong — and having no disguise about him, both appeared in full force. — He was generous & disinterested — but plain and blunt in his manner even to rudeness."[94] Whatever his large or small disagreements with England, he respected character and ability when he saw it.

Moreover, Washington did not boast about his own courage, although his actions demonstrated that he was indeed brave. Describing the ambush of Braddock's troops, he simply noted that he had had "one horse killed, and two wounded under him — a ball through his hat — and several through his clothes but escaped unhurt."[95] Although he discussed a tour of the frontier forts which nearly resulted in his being captured, he did not mention the threat to his own personal safety.[96] His comments confirm that even in private, Washington was not a presumptuous or self-important person. He could understate his bravery because it was so obvious.

Although Washington gave a fairly straightforward account of his actions, his statements were notable for their omissions. Washington, for example, failed to mention the enormous controversy following the surrender at Fort Necessity, where he had unwittingly signed a document admitting that he had assassinated the French leader, Ensign Jumonville.[97] Nor did he mention his vigorous opposition to Forbes's plan for cutting a new road to Fort Duquesne. Washington's strategy very well may have led to disaster, while Forbes's plan resulted in victory.[98] Perhaps, as Washington claimed, he was merely suffering from "the badness of his Memory."[99] Whether the omissions were intentional or not, the effect was to produce a more flattering picture of the general than if he had mentioned them.

Historians have often referred to Washington's "aloofness"; to his "mysterious[ness]"; to the perception that "he was a stranger, in his inmost self, to those around him." [100] His "Remarks," however, reveals a less elusive Washington. In his comments the general openly expressed his reactions to past events, even when they were painful or traumatic. Writing about the aftermath of the Braddock ambush, he described the carnage in terms that reveal a frightened young man much more than a hardened war veteran. "The shocking scenes which presented themselves in this Nights march," he said, "are not to be described—The dead—the dying—the groans—lamentations—and crys along the Road of the wounded for help . . . were enough to pierce a heart of adamant.— The gloom & horror of which was not a little increased by the impervious darkness occasioned by the close shade of thick woods which in places rendered it impossible for the two guides which attended to know when they were in, or out of the track but by groping on the ground with their hands." [101] He remembered his poignant leave-taking during the French and Indian War. The troops' "affectionate farewell address to him . . . affected him exceedingly and in grateful sensibility he expressed the warmth of his attachment to them on that, and his inclination to serve them on every other future occasion." [102] Although Washington may have felt the need to maintain a formal distance between himself and his troops, that aloofness did not indicate a lack of feeling for those who served under him.

The most important passage in the autobiographical "Remarks" was also the most personally revealing. In his discussion of the French and Indian War, Washington included a recollection of a devastating incident that he reported nowhere else in his correspondence or papers.[103] On November 12, 1758, the British were pressing northward toward Fort Duquesne in a desperate effort to beat the onset of winter. The lookouts sent word that the French were approaching their position at Loyal Hannon, determined to raid British cattle and horses. According to Washington, Lieutenant Colonel Mercer and his troops had been sent to deter the enemy and became embroiled in a prolonged exchange of fire. When it appeared that the British were losing ground, Washington received General Forbes's permission to march with reinforcements to Mercer's aid. But it was near evening and, according to one account, a "remarkably dark and foggy" day.[104] Tragedy soon struck. Coming within half a mile of the shooting, Washington recalled that he

> detached Scouts . . . to communicate his approach to his friend Colonel Mercer advancing slowly in the meantime — But it being near dusk and the intelligence not having been fully dissiminated among Colonel Mercers Corps, and they taking us, for the enemy who had retreated approaching in another direction commenced a heavy fire upon the relieving party which drew fire in return in spite of all the exertions of the Officers one of whom & several privates were killed and many wounded before a stop could be put to it. To accomplish which George Washington never was in more imminent danger by being between two fires, knocking up with his sword the presented pieces.[105]

The volley between Washington's and Mercer's men resulted in the death of at least fourteen men and in the wounding of many others.

Washington's account differed from other contemporary versions in some important regards. There were differences in the number of people reported killed and wounded, as well as discrepancies in the stated sequence of events. Most important, while Washington remembered going to the aid of Mercer, the *Pennsylvania Gazette* of November 30, 1758, reported that Mercer was sent to assist Washington.[106] Whatever the precise facts, however, Washington's feelings about the incident were

clear enough. His fear, grief, and sense of personal responsi-
bility were still palpable thirty years later. The dangers he had
encountered as commander-in-chief paled in comparison with
an episode that he said had put his life "in as much jeopardy as
it had ever been before or since." [107] Only after three decades
could Washington bear to write about it—and then only to his
trusted friend David Humphreys.

Washington's "Remarks" thus constitutes an important and
unique source for understanding the general. It modifies in
some important ways the conventional stereotype of Washington as a man and as a military leader. He appears more emo-
tional and less stoic: more self-righteous about his causes, more
sentimental toward his men, and more sensitive to the horrors
of war. This Washington, while possessing all the bravery and
integrity usually ascribed to him, also appears fully human. [108]

The Washington of
"The Life of General Washington"

Just as Washington's notes deepen our understanding of the
general, so too does the biography that Humphreys wrote. The
colonel, in fact, seems to have realized that his distinctive con-
tribution lay in his understanding of Washington as a private
citizen. "The virtuous simplicity which distinguishes the private life of General Washington," he said, "though less known
than the dazzling splendour of his military atcheivments, is not
less edifying in example & ought not to be less interesting to his
countrymen." [109] "In proportion," he continued, "as his private
as well as his public life shall be more known, a higher opinion
will be entertained of his character." [110] Humphreys specifically
eschewed a detailed discussion of Washington's Revolutionary

War exploits "because the impression which he made is yet fresh in every mind." [111] He aimed to emphasize the private side of the well-known figure.

Because of his intimacy with Washington, Humphreys provided insights and observations that no other biographer could offer. Washington, he said, had received his early education from a private tutor. Except for the entreaties of his mother, he would have joined the British navy.[112] Washington was proud of his physical prowess. The general, he said, claimed that he had "never met with any man who could throw a stone to so great a distance as himself; and, that when standing in the valley beneath the natural bridge in Virginia, he has thrown one up to that stupendous arch." [113] His interests and pastimes changed over time. By 1788, Humphreys said, Washington had lost his passion for his favorite sport, foxhunting.[114] His moods, while predictable, did shift. After retiring to Mount Vernon, Humphreys noted, Washington was "more chearful than he was in the army. Notwithstanding his temper is rather of a serious cast & his countenance commonly carries the impression of thoughtfulness; he perfectly relishes a pleasant story, an unaffected sally of wit, or a burlesque description which surprises by its suddenness & incongruity with the ordinary appearance of the same object." [115]

Humphreys' most important revelation concerned the general's long and agonizing battle over whether to accept the presidency. At the end of the Revolution, Washington had made a dramatic gesture in resigning his commission. Claiming that his work was done, he said that he desired to return to private life and leave the governing of the country to others. But as soon as the federal Constitution was unveiled, public opinion immediately rallied behind Washington as the choice for the first president. Even before ratification, newspapers and private individuals insisted that Washington was the only one who could unite the country and put the new government into operation.[116]

Washington, however, wanted no part of these speculations. He enjoyed his retirement at Mount Vernon and felt he could not reverse his decision to remain in private life. He detested public scrutiny and abhorred the suggestion that he possessed personal ambitions to serve in high public office.[117] He insisted that many others were better qualified than he to be president. In a letter to Alexander Hamilton dated October 3, 1788, he asserted:

> Situated as I am, I could hardly bring the question into the slightest discussion, or ask an opinion even in the most confidential manner; without betraying, in my judgment, some impropriety of conduct, or without feeling an apprehension, that a premature display of anxiety, might be construed into a vainglorious desire of pushing myself into notice as a Candidate. Now, if I am not grossly deceived in myself, I should unfeignedly rejoice, in case the Electors, by giving their votes in favor of some other person, would save me from the dreaded Dilemma of being forced to accept or refuse.[118]

Even as late as January 1789, a month before his formal election and three months before he took office, Washington still refused to reveal publicly his decision. He even kept close friends guessing.[119]

Humphreys' biography allows us to see Washington's struggle from the inside, from the perspective of a person who was both a witness to and a participant in the affair. Recounting conversations with Washington, Humphreys revealed the genuine indecision that plagued Washington. Although attracted by the honor, Washington felt bound to abide by his word and remain a private citizen. Although pleased by the attention, he shrank from even the vaguest appearance of impropriety or self-promotion. Humphreys recounted an incident that revealed how sensitive Washington was about the subject. In June 1788 the citizens of Baltimore sent Washington a gift, the miniature ship *Federalist*, built to celebrate their state's ratification of the Constitution. Washington's immediate response was to fear that acceptance of the gift would imply his expectation of "being employed in the federal government." [120] Humphreys insisted that Washington should accept the present, arguing that the ship was "intended only as a mark of respect, & without being meant as a scheme for drawing any conclusion with regard to the General's future conduct." [121] Humphreys' arguments seem to have convinced Washington. He graciously accepted the people's token of appreciation.[122]

Although Washington may have been above self-promotion, Humphreys was not. Humphreys claimed that he played a pivotal role in persuading Washington to accept the presidency. "The first conversation which General Washington ever held with any person on the question of his accepting or refusing the Office of the President of the United States," he said, "was with the Author of this work." [123] According to Humphreys, Washington had at that point, "resolved to decline accepting the Office." [124] Reasoning thus, Washington told Humphreys that "after having made known [my] intentions of remaining in private life, [I] should cirtainly be reproached with glaring inconsistency for having departed from those declarations: That [I] must also incur the imputation of acting from motives of ambition: and therefore . . . by accepting the appointment [I would] injure the interests of the new government, rather than lend any aid toward a quiet acquiescence in it." [125] Humphreys, however, claimed that he convinced the general to delay his decision until the post was actually offered to him.

Humphreys' first conversation with Washington about the presidency, lasting four hours, occurred in June 1788 — long before he had confided in any of his other confidants. Subsequently, Humphreys said, he and the general discussed the subject nearly every day.[126] In later conversations Humphreys turned the full range of his persuasive skills on his mentor. "Perhaps it will be found," he said, "that the very existence of the government will be much endangered, if the person placed at the Head of it should not possess the entire confidence of both its friends & adversaries."[127] He tried to have Washington see the positive as well as the negative aspects of his position. "From all the treatment you have ever experienced from the people of this Continent you have a right to believe, that they entertain a good opinion of your abilities—That they entertain a superlatively high opinion of your prudence, integrity & disinterestedness. . . . You ought, at sometimes, Sir, to look upon the bright side of the picture; and not always to be pondering the objects you find on the Reverse."[128] He concluded his exhortation saying, "If, after having seen your country placed in a situation, capable of enjoying all the public felicity which is incident to the lot of humanity, you shall be at liberty to retire again to domestic life; you may congratulate yourself upon having been at last the most fortunate, the most favored, of mortals."[129]

It is impossible to know the precise effect of Humphreys' words on Washington. Egotistical as he was, Humphreys certainly had a stake in highlighting his own role in convincing the general to accept the position. But many of Washington's other friends and acquaintances also told him the same thing. Alexander Hamilton, Benjamin Lincoln, the marquis de Lafayette and others wrote numerous letters insisting on the necessity of Washington's accepting the position to help ensure the success of the new government.[130] Yet Humphreys' physical presence at Mount Vernon and his active support of the cause may have reinforced what the others were saying. It may have given Washington the strength he needed to make an extremely difficult decision. "If my appointment & acceptance be inevitable," he told Humphreys, "I fear I must bid adieu to happiness, for I see nothing, but clouds & darkness before me: and I call God to witness that the day which shall carry me again into public life, will be a more distressing one than any I have ever yet known." [131]

Whatever Humphreys' role in getting the general to accept the presidency, his biography fleshes out our understanding of Washington the man. Washington genuinely agonized over whether to accept the nation's highest office, debating the subject endlessly with Humphreys. He was not merely expressing his insecurities in the hope of being flattered, nor was he attempting to be coy. Concerned about the substance as well as the appearance of impropriety, he feared not only for his own reputation but for the future of the country that he had helped to found. Today people automatically suspect the worst about politicians and doubt the sincerity of their emotions. Humphreys' account, however, proves that the first president was a man of integrity. He expressed the same sentiments to his confidants as to his casual acquaintances; he was the same person in private as in public.

In 1943 the literary critic Leon Howard published *The Connecticut Wits*, in which he rendered a harsh and unsympathetic assessment of Humphreys' career. Unaware that Humphreys had succeeded in writing the Washington biography, Howard mused sarcastically about the potential impact of such a work. "Had Humphreys," he said, "with his unconscious ability to invoke the attraction of myths for the simple [people], gone on to make another study of Washington, the world might have had a narrative so remarkable that even Parson Weems' cherry tree would have been lost in the enchanted forest." [132]

But Howard was wrong. Humphreys had surpassed himself in writing his "Life of General Washington." Unlike Weems's caricature of George Washington, Humphreys' Washington was a real person—a man sickened by the screams of his wounded troops, touched by the appeals of his subordinates, piqued by those who had crossed him, and tormented about whether to accept the presidency. He liked to hunt foxes, drink madeira, and listen to jokes made by his friends. While it is certainly true that Humphreys wanted his Washington to symbolize values that were larger than life, his Washington lived life to the fullest. It is hard after reading Humphreys' account to see the first president as either an aloof stick-figure or an earnest do-gooder. The Humphreys biography humanizes Washington without trivializing him. Even more important, it humanizes him in terms that a contemporary provided, without the gloss of subsequent centuries.

It *is* interesting to compare the impact of Humphreys' biography with the nearly contemporaneous biography of Washington by Parson Weems. Humphreys' and Weems's biographies were similar in important ways: both portrayed Washington as a model of civic virtue whose private life was as exemplary as his public deeds.[133] Yet Weems did not know Washington personally. What he did not know about the general he simply made up. Washington's purported felling of a cherry tree is the most famous, but by no means the only, example of Weems's fabrications. Humphreys' work, on the other hand, was far more accurate, based on Humphreys' first-hand observations of and conversations with Washington. Accuracy, however, did not ensure popularity. The part of Humphreys' biography published during his lifetime never achieved the fame or enduring success of Weems's version. Perhaps Humphreys' account was too prosaic—and not mythic enough—to gain widespread approval.

History, as we know, gives people a way of understanding themselves, providing continuity and a sense of collective identity amidst change. At different times and places, people seek out different themes in their history. In the early years of the nation, Americans may have needed Weems's Washington—a man who never told lies, who constantly testified to the tenets of Christianity, and whose mother dreamed of her son's future role in leading the republic. Today, however, Humphreys' Washington may have more appeal. The colonel's account suggests that Washington was a man whose bravery needed no comment, a politician who was as good as his word, and a leader whose integrity was as apparent in his private life as in his public deeds. Because Humphreys' Washington didn't cut down a cherry tree, he had no need to lie about it.

Editorial Statement

THE CURRENT WORK represents the first modern edition of
David Humphreys' unfinished "Life of General Washington."
Some of the material has not been published since Humphreys'
lifetime; other parts have never before been published. It is
the first time all the existing parts of the biography have been
published in one place. The edition attempts to construct a co-
herent and readable version of the biography while at the same
time remaining true to what Humphreys actually wrote. It is
necessarily a "critical" or "eclectic" text because no one of the
three manuscripts alone is comprehensive or complete.[1] The
intention is to produce the biography that Humphreys would
have written had he finished the project.

In manuscript form the biography remains virtually inacces-
sible to readers. The "Life of Washington" is scattered amidst
Humphreys' notes in papers held by three different archives.
One part, which covers the period from Washington's birth
to his retirement after the Revolution, is in the collection of
the Rosenbach Museum and Library in Philadelphia.[2] A second manuscript, at the Yale University Library, consists of
earlier drafts of some of the material found in the Rosenbach
as well as an entirely new section concerned with Washington's life from the time of the federal constitutional convention until his assumption of the presidency.[3] A third document,
called Washington's "Remarks," consisting of Washington's

notes and comments on the Humphreys manuscript, is in the *Forbes Magazine* Collection, New York City.[4] As a conclusion to Humphreys' otherwise unfinished work, I have added to this edition an epilogue that Humphreys wrote to his "Poem on the Death of General Washington." The epilogue is contained in a copybook among Humphreys' papers at Yale.[5]

The edition has several distinct sections. The "Life of Washington" proper, based on my reconstruction of the text, follows the Introduction and Editorial Statement. I have collated the various versions of the manuscript and tried to provide a smooth chronological rendering of Washington's life. Washington's notes have been inserted into the text and are indicated by the use of angle brackets: ⟨*GW note:* . . . ⟩. Although Washington often placed a footnote in mid-sentence, for the sake of readability the notes have been placed at the end of the sentence or phrase to which they refer. In addition, I have eliminated Washington's footnote numbers, which might be confused with the notes to this edition. In order to signal significant breaks in the narrative, I have inserted a line of asterisks. References to the manuscript sources, variant readings of the text, and historical commentary are contained in the Notes. Because the Introduction discusses literary and historical matters in detail, the substantive notes to the "Life" are kept to a minimum and are meant to complete, clarify, or correct the text. The next part of the edition consists of a section called "Outlines and Non-Biographical Material," which contains the material remaining in Humphreys' notes after the extraction of the Washington biography. Much of it is directly relevant to Washington, including Humphreys' outlines of the proposed biography. It also contains parts of letters and speeches written by Humphreys for Washington. One kind of entry has not been reproduced in full. Humphreys included many lengthy book summaries in his notes. Rather than reproduce these summaries, I have simply cited the works in question. Although I have been able to identify titles and authors, it has not always been possible to locate the exact editions to which Humphreys referred. In these cases, I have cited other editions available at the time.

Editing the Humphreys manuscript was in many ways like doing an elaborate puzzle. The numerous additions, deletions, and interlineations indicate that the manuscript was a working draft. Humphreys wrote about Washington in the same notebooks—many times even on the same pages—that he wrote speeches, letters, essays, and book summaries. The Washington biography is buried among these other writings. As editor, I had to determine which materials were or were not part of the biography, a choice that was usually, but not always, obvious. A further problem was to figure out how the pieces all fit together. Often pages ended in mid-sentence. At times, Humphreys included catchwords (the last word of the previous page repeated as the first word of the next page) that allowed the reader to see which page came next. At other times he was not so considerate, and the sense of the sentence had to determine what came next. The order of the parts was also problematic. Humphreys apparently did not write the biography in chronological order, although it is apparent from the outlines that he intended it to proceed in that fashion. It was thus necessary to put the pieces into the correct order on the basis of the outlines Humphreys provided and from a knowledge of Washington's life.

Although both Washington and Humphreys had handwriting that is generally easy to read, their insertions, deletions, and interlineations sometimes made interpreting their handwriting quite difficult. I have chosen not to transcribe all of the crossed-out words and sections because I believe they would make the text more confusing and less readable. Moreover, because my focus is more on an accessible version of Humphreys' biography, and less on the thought processes that led Humphreys or Washington to that point, I do not feel the exclusion of deleted material detracts from the project's value.

The manuscripts contain a fair number of insertions. When Humphreys or Washington indicated that an item should be inserted on the same page, I have included the material without comment. But in cases where Humphreys or Washington wanted an insertion to be made from one page to another, I have recorded this fact in the Notes. In the few instances where the authors failed to indicate where an insertion belonged, I have included it at the most appropriate place and so stated in a note. In a related matter, Humphreys often rewrote the same text several times, using slightly different words or phrases. He frequently failed to indicate which reading he preferred. I have presented what seems to have been the first (or failing that, the most polished) version. I have reproduced the other versions as so-called "alternate readings" in the Notes.

In general, the authors' spelling, capitalization, paragraphing, and punctuation have been retained. Changes or additions made for the sake of readability have been inserted in brackets. All abbreviations and contractions (when obvious from the context) have been silently expanded. The ampersand, however, has been retained. Catchwords have not been repeated. Blank spaces within a line are indicated by the word *blank* in brackets. No attempt has been made to reproduce accurately the number of blank spaces or blank lines. All dashes, whatever their length in the written manuscript, have been reproduced as one-em (−) dashes. Horizontal lines separating one fragment from another are not reproduced in the body of the Washington biography but are included in the Outlines and Non-Biographical Material. Many words and phrases in the original manuscripts were underlined. Humphreys seemed fond of underlining parts of the text for reasons that are not apparent to the modern reader. These passages (with the exception of foreign words) have been regularized without comment. Washington, however, appeared to use underlining to add emphasis; in his "Remarks" underlined words have been italicized.

References to page numbers also presented a problem. Some pages in the Rosenbach manuscript are numbered, presumably by Humphreys, but the numbering is neither consistent nor complete. The Rosenbach curators have penciled in their own numbers, and these are the numbers I have used. The major Yale manuscript consists of forty-four loose pages, which are not numbered. I have assigned numbers to the pages and provided an Appendix in which I have listed the first words on each of my numbered pages. Both Humphreys' copybook at Yale and Washington's "Remarks" have numbers in the upper right-hand corner of each page. These are the numbers to which I refer in those manuscripts.

David Humphreys'
"Life of General Washington"
with George Washington's "Remarks"

"The Life of General Washington" by David Humphreys, with George Washington's "Remarks"

THERE ARE CERTAIN EPOCHAS in the annals of mankind, which, being capable of gratifying a rational curiosity on account of events uncommon in their nature as interesting in their consequence, serve as so many stages for the mind to rest upon, while it is journeying in speculation through the more barren ages that have elapsed since the creation of this habitable globe.[1] Such are periods made memorable by the rise, the revolution or the fall of empires. The revolution which has recently been effected in North America, & which has changed an appendage of the British empire, consisting of thirteen flourishing Colonies, into a Confederacy of thirteen independent States, will long possess the advantage of attracting the notice of the world in general; as well as of marking an era of unrivalled importance to the People of this Continent in particular. Insomuch that no material occurrence attended its commencement,[2] progress, & termination [it] can contribute to form an inspired page in the volume of human history. Nor can the conduct & characters of those persons, who were illustrious instruments in the hand of Providence for estab-

lishing the Independence of the new World, be objects un-
worthy of attention. Posterity, it may naturally be concluded,
will contemplate with singular delight & admiration the pic-
tures of those patriots which shall have been faithfully drawn
by the hand of a Contemporary. The portrait of the person,
who commanded the troops of the Union during the whole
term of that perilous struggle, & who afterwards assisted in
securing the fruits of the revolution, of right, stand promi-
nent in the glorious groupe.[3] It is therefore my intention to
employ my pen in preserving such circumstances[4] relative to
himself & the public transactions in which he was concerned,
as have come to my knowledge.[5] It is remarkable that none of
the professional scribblers have presumed to sully the bright-
ness or vilify the grandeur of the Original, by giving (at full
length) instead of a just likeness, a monstrous caricature in
their unskilled dawbings. On a matter of such expectation, the
difficulty of succeeding to the satisfaction of the Public, which
may even have deterred some abler Authors from[6] handling the
subject, seems to require an apology for the present attempt.
To the Writer of these memoirs on General Washington, a
consciousness of possessing an uncommon share in his confidence &, in many instances, a full knowledge of his motives,
together with a promise from him of whatever manuscript or
oral communications were necessary, might have been no inconsiderable inducements to have hazarded the undertaking.
But the General's opinion, that the writer was more competent
in several respects to the execution of the task than any other,
could not fail of being decisive with the latter. Should he be
so happy as to preserve any hitherto unwritten materials for
history from the voraciousness of consuming time or to res-
cue any official documents from the profanation of mercenary
hands, the Youth of America, unborn at the time when these

events took place, will have some occasion to applaud the design. And should the success be in proportion to the subject—future Generations will rejoice at finding in one[7] point of view so many facts relative to a man, who received, while living, the unlimited applause of his Countrymen; to whose memory, when dead, the incense of gratitude will not cease to be offerred; and whose examples of private morality will forever be cited by parents for the imitation of their sons—: Nor need we fear to predict, that, so long as the imperial fabric which he hath assisted to raise shall endure, heroes will be proud to emulate his military virtues, senates continue to inculcate the practice of his political precepts, and infants be taught to lisp the name of their country's benefactor in the first efforts of articulation.[8]

The birth of George Washington the late Commander in Chief of the American forces, & the first President of the United States under the reformed Constitution, happened on the [*blank*] of February 1734 Old Style,[9] in the Parish of Washington, near Pope's Creek, on the southern bank of the river Potowmac, and at about [*blank*] miles distance from Richmond, the present Capital of Virginia.[10] His Ancestors who transferred a considerable inheritance from their native to their adoptive country, had been in the new World from the year 1657—When two brothers, whose names were John & Lawrence & whose descendents have since greatly multiplied came to America over the Atlantic from Cumberland in England. Almost every branch of their offspring still possesses a considerable portion of property & respectability. Augustine Washington, the immediate progenitor of him whose life is the subject of this disertation, was descended from the elder house, in the second generation after the migration to America. By his first wife, Jane Butler, he had four children, none of whom arrived at middle age: by his second marriage with Mary Ball (a respectable matron still living) he had six other children — of these the subject of this history was the oldest.[11]

Education] His father and two oldest brothers had received their education in England; whither he would have been sent for the same purpose had it not been for the death of the former who had made several voyages to that country. This was the common mode of disposing of the children of opulent families. For such as were brought up at home were in danger of becoming indolent & helpless from the usual indulgence giving a horse & a servant to attend them, as soon as they could ride; if not imperious & dissipated from the habit of commanding slaves & living in a measure without controul. Those Virginians, educated in a domestic manner, who had fortitude enough to resist the temptations to which they were exposed in their youth, have commonly been distinguished by success in their various professions. Many Virginians, besides him whose life is here intended to be discussed, are the most remarkable examples of application & perseverance, which this age has produced.[12]

The aid of patrimonial provision for the second Son would be sufficient to bring him forward in the world with advantage: without encouraging, however, that indolent repose on an expected fortune, which, in countries where the distribution of money is altogether unequal, has ruined many a pregnant & promising young genius.[13] By a domestic tutor (which was then generally & is now frequently the mode of education practiced in that part of the Continent) he was betimes instructed in the principles of grammar, the theory of reasoning, on speaking, the science of numbers, the elements of geometry, & the highest branches of mathematics, the art of mensuration, composing together with the rudiments of geography, history & the studies which are not improperly termed "the humanities."

In the graceful accomplishments[14] of dancing, fencing, riding & performing the military exercises he likewise made an early & conspicuous proficiency. In short, he was carefully initiated into whatever might be most useful to him, in making his way to preferment in the British army or navy, for which he was designed.[15]

Though he was rather unsure & reserved in his appearance; he was frequently animated & fluent in conversation & always descreed[16] in conduct. & In the performance of any business committed to him, he was active, indefatigable, persevering. [He was noted for] His tall stature, for he was clear six feet high without his shoes; his gentiel deportment, for he had something uncommonly noble in his manners; his modest behaviour, which, without being the result of ill-becoming diffidence[.][17]

[He was] remarkably robust & athletic. I have several times heard him say, he never met any man who could throw a stone to so great a distance as himself; and, that when standing in the valley beneath the natural bridge in Virginia, he has thrown one up to that stupendous arch.

[H]unting & surveying—the first gave him activity & boldness—the second the means of improving the *Coup d'oeil* in judging of military positions & measuring by the eye the distance between different places.— Patience & perseverance in reconnoitring—how often he spent whole days on horseback, braving the ravages of the most violent heat & cold that ever was experienced in our climate.[18]

As it was the design of his Father that he should be bred for an Officer in the British navy, his mental acquisitions & exterior accomplishments were calculated to give him distinction in that profession. ⟨*GW note:* It was rather the wish of my eldest brother (on whom the several concerns of the family devolved) that this should take place & the matter was contemplated by him— My father died when I was only 10 years old.¹⁹⟩ At 15 years old, he was entered a midshipman on board of the [*blank*] & his baggage prepared for embarkation:²⁰ but the plan was abandoned in consequence of the earnest solicitations of his Mother.²¹

The Father of General Washington had three sons by a former wife. The eldest, a young man of the most promising talents, after having been appointed Adjutant General of the Militia of Virginia, commanded the Colonial troops in the expedition against Carthagena; ⟨*GW note:* He was not appointed Adjutant General of the Militia of Virginia until after his return from the expedition to Carthagena.— Nor did he command the Colonial troops at that occasion. These were under the orders of Sir William Gouch Lieutenant Governor of Virginia—He was no more than the Senior Officer of those which were raised in this Colony & which with those of the other Colonies formed what was called the American Brigade—under Sir William Gouch—he was scarcely of age when he went on this expedition.²²⟩ and on his return called his patrimonial Mansion, Mount Vernon, in honour of the Admiral of that name with whom he had contracted a particular intimacy. ⟨*GW note:* And from whom he had received many distinguished marks of patronage & favor.²³⟩ On the death of all the children by the first marriage, General Washington acceded²⁴ to a large landed property: ⟨*GW note:* Not all—for the second Son (Augustine) left many children, several of whom are now living; and inherit a very large portion of his Fathers Estate. perhaps the best part.²⁵⟩ in consequence of the vacancy in the Office of Adjutant General & of the extensive limits of the Colony, the Office was divided into three districts, and the future hero of America began his military career by a principal appointment in that Department, with the rank of Major.²⁶ ⟨*GW note:* Before he was 20 years of age.²⁷⟩ He had previously shewn the tenderest affection to his eldest brother during his declining health & attended him to the West Indies a little before his death. This was the only time that ever General Washington was from the Continent of America.[28]

When he was little more than twenty one years of age, an event occurred, which called his abilities into public notice. ⟨*GW note:* He was then more than 21 years — as will appear from dates.[29]⟩ In the year 1753, while the government of the Colony was administered by Lieutenant Governor Dinwiddie, Encroachments were reported to have been made by the French from Canada on the territories of the British Colonies at the westward and a Post about to be established at the confluence of the Ohio & Monongahela, then called fort du Quesne, now well-known by the name of fort Pitt. Young Mr Washington, who, was sent with plenary powers to ascertain the facts, to treat with the Savages, and to warn the French to desist from their aggressions, performed the duties of his Mission with singular[30] industry, intelligence & address. ⟨*GW note:* At a most inclement Season, for he travelled over the Apalachean Mountains, and passed 250 Miles thro an uninhabited wilderness country (except by a few tribes of Indians settled on the Banks of the Ohio) to Presque Isle within 15 miles of Lake Erie in the depth of the winter when the whole face of the Earth was covered with snow and the waters covered with Ice; — The whole distance from Williamsburgh the then seat of Government at least 500 miles. — [31]⟩ His Journal of proceedings, & official Report to Governor Dinwiddie, which were published, announced to the world that correctness of mind, manliness in style, and accuracy in the mode of doing business, which have since rendered him so illustrious in more arduous affairs.[32] But it was deemed by some an extraordinary circumstance that so young and inexperienced a Person should have been employed on a negotiation, with which subjects of the greatest importance were involved; subjects which shortly after became the origin of a war between the two Kingdoms of England & France, that raged for many years throughout every part of the world. ⟨*GW note:* It was on this occasion he was named by the half-King (as he was called) and the tribes of Nations with whom he treated—Caunotaucarius (in English) the Towntaker; which name being registered in their Manner & communicated to other Nations of Indians, has been remembered by them ever since in all their transactions with him during the late War.— [33]⟩

These troubles still subsisting & encreasing on the frontiers; the Colony of Virginia, resolved, the next year, to levy a Regiment of Troops for their defence. Of this Corps, Mr Fry, one of the Professors of the College of William & Mary, an aged & inactive man, but supposed to be theoretically acquainted with tactics & encampments, was appointed Colonel; and Major Washington, whose resource & alertness were expected to compensate for the defects of those qualities in the former, received the Commission of Leiutenant Colonel. But Colonel Fry died the same summer, without having ever joined his[34] Regiment, and, of course, left the command & rank to the Leiutenant Colonel.[35]

II (NB. here General Washington is requested by David Humphreys to give, in brief, some few of the most interesting facts relative to this & the subsequent campaigns, viz., the action at the great Meadows—the seige & surrender of fort Necessity—with other occurrences until Braddock's death—and indeed to annex similiar accounts after Braddock's defeat untill his own leaving the service; if there should be any thing particularly worthy of preservation; according to the minute scale, on which this specimen of biography is intended)[36] ⟨*GW note:* This is a task to which George Washington feels himself very incompetent (with any degree of accuracy) from the badness of his memory—loss of Papers—mutilated state in which those of that date were preserved—and the derangement of them by frequent removals in the late war & want of time to collect and methodize them since.— However according to the best of his recollection: by the indefatigable Industry of the Lieutenant Colonel and the Officers who [37] seconded his measures the Regiment was in great forwardness at Alexandria (the place of general Rendezvous) early in the spring of 1754. Without waiting till the whole should be compleated—or for a detachment from the Independant Companies of Regulars in the Southern Provences (which had been requested by the Executive of Virginia for this service) or for troops which were raising in North Carolina and destined in conjunction to oppose the Incroachment of the French on our Western frontiers—He began his March in the Month of May in order to open the Road and this he had to do almost the whole distance *from Winchester* (in the County of Frederick not more than 80 miles from Alexandria to the Ohio)—For deposits—etc.—and for the especiall purpose of seizing, if possible, before the French should arrive at it, the important Post at the conflux of the Alligany and Monongahela, with the advantages of which he was forcibly struck the preceeding year; and earnestly advised the securing of with Militia, or some other temporary force. But notwithstanding all his exertions, the New, and uncommon difficulties he had to encounter (made more intolerable by incessant Rains and swelled waters of which he had many to cross) he had but just ascended the Laurel Hill 50 Miles short of his object, after a March of 230 miles from Alexandria when he received information from his Scouts that the French had in force, siezed the Post he was pushing to obtain; having descended from Presque Isle by the Rivers Lebeuf and Alligany to this Place by water with Artillery, &c. The object of his precipitate advance being thus defeated—The detachment of regulars which had arrived at Alexandria (by water) and under his orders being far in his rear and no Account of the Troops from North Carolina — it was thought advisable to fall back a few miles, to a place known by the name of the great Meadows — abounding in Forage and more convenient for the purpose of forming a Magazine & bringing up the Rear — and to advance from (if we should ever be in force to do it) to the attack of the Post which the enemy now occupied, and had called Du Quesne — At this place, some days after we were joined by the above detachment of Regulars, consisting (before they were reduced on the March by [38] desertion, Sickness &c.) of a Captain McKay (a brave & worthy officer), three Subalterns, and 100 Rank & file. — But previous to this junction the French sent a detachment to reconnoitre our Camp & to obtain intelligence of our strength & position, notice of which being given by the Scouts George Washington marched at the head of a party, attacked, killed 9 or 10, & captured 20 odd. — This, as soon as the enemy had assembled their Indian Allies, brought their whole force upon him, consisting according to their own compared with the best account that could be obtained from others of about 1500 Men. His force consisted of the detachment above mentioned, and between two & 300 Virginians, for the few Indians which till now had attended him, and who by reconnoitering the enemy in their march had got terrified at their numbers and resolved to retreat as they advised us to do also but which was impracticable without abandoning our Stores — Baggage — &c.: as the horses which had brought them to this place had returned for Provision had left us previous to the Attack. About 9 oclock on the 3d of July the Enemy advanced with Shouts, & dismal Indian yells to our Intrenchments, but was opposed by so warm, spirited & constant a fire, that to force the works in *that way* was abandoned by them. They then, from every little rising tree —

stump—stone—and bush kept up a constant galding fire upon us, which was returned in the best manner we could till late in the afternoon when their fell the most tremendous rain that can be conceived—filled our trenches with water—wet, not only the ammunition in the Cartooch boxes and firelocks, but that which was in a small temporary Stockade in the middle of the Intrenchment called Fort Necessity erected for the sole purpose of its security, and that of the few stores we had, and left us nothing but a few (for all were not provided with them) Bayonets for defence.— In this situation [with] *no* prospect of bettering it terms of capitulation were offered to us by the enemy which with some alterations that were insisted upon were the more readily acceded to, as we had no Salt provisions, & but indifferently supplied with fresh [foods], which, from the heat of the weather, would not keep, and because a full third of our numbers, officers as well as privates were, by this time, killed or wounded—The next Morning we marched out with the honors of War, but were [39] plundered, contrary to the Articles of capitulation of great part of our Baggage by the Savages.— Our Sick and wounded were left with a detachment under the care, and command of the worthy Doctor Craik (for he was not only Surgeon to the Regiment but a lieutenant therein) with such necessities as we could collect and the Remains of the Regiment, and the detachment of Regulars, took up their line for the interior Country.— [40] And at Winchester met 2 Companies from North Carolina on their March to join them—These being fresh, & properly provided, were ordered to proceed to Will's Creek & establish a post (since called Fort Cumberland) for the purpose of covering the Frontiers, Where they were joined by a Company from Maryland, which about this time, had been raized—Captain McKay with his detachment removed at Winchester, & the Virginia Regiment proceeded to Alexandria in order to recruit, & get supplied with cloathing & necessarys of which they stood much in need. In this manner the Winter was employed, when advice was received of the force destined for this Service under the orders of General Braddock and the arrival of Sir Jonathan St. Clair the Quartermaster General with some new arrangement of Rank by which no officer who did not *immediately* derive his Commission from the *King* could command one *who did* — This was too degrading for George Washington to submit to; accordingly, he resigned his Military employment, determining to serve the next campaign as a Volunteer; but upon the arrival of General Braddock he was very particularly noticed by that General — taken into his family as an extra-Aid — offered a Captains Commission by *brevet* (which was the highest Grade he had it in his power to bestow) and had the compliment of several blank Ensigncies given to him to dispose of to the young gentlemen of his acquaintance to supply the vacancies in the 44 and 48 Regiments which had arrived from Ireland.

In this capacity he commenced his second Campaign, and used every proper occasion till he was taken sick & left behind in the vicinity of Fort Cumberland to impress the General, & the principal Officers around him, with the necessity of opposing the nature of his defence, to the mode of attack which, more than probably he would experience from the *Canadian* French, and their *Indians* on his March through the Mountains & covered Country but so prepossessed were they in favor of *regularity* & *discipline* and in such absolute contempt were *these people held*, that the admonition was suggested in vain. — [41]

About the middle of June, this Armament consisting of the two Regiments from Ireland — some Independant Companies and the Provincial troops of Virginia Maryland & North Carolina began to move from Fort Cumberland whither they had assembled — after several days March, and difficulties to which they had never been accustomed in Regular Service, in Champaign Countries, and of which they seemed to have had very little idea—the General resolved to divide his force, and at the head of the first division which was composed of the flower of his Army, to advance; and leave Colonel Dunbar with the second division & the heavy Baggage & stores, to follow after.— By so doing, the first division approached the Monongahela 10 miles short of Fort Duquesne the 8th of July; at which time, and place having so far recovered from a severe fever and delerium from which he had been rescued by James's powder, administered by the positive order of the General as to travel in a covered Waggon, he joined him and the next day tho' much reduced and very weak mounted his horse on cushions, & attended as one of his aids.—

About 10 oclock on the 9th, after the Van had crossed the Monongahela the *second time*, to avoid an ugly defilement (the season being very dry & waters low) and the Rear yet in the River the front was attacked; and by the unusual Hallooing and whooping of the enemy, whom they could not see, were so disconcerted and confused as soon to fall into irretrievable disorder.— The Rear was forced forward to support them, but seeing no enemy, and themselves falling every moment from the fire, a general panic took place among the Troops from which no exertions of the Officers could recover them—In the early part of the Action some of the Irregulars (as they were called) *without directions* advanced to the right, in loose order, to attack; but this, *unhappily*, from the unusual appearance of the movement being mistaken for cowardice and running away was discountenanced—and before it was *too late*, & the confusion became general an offer was made by George Washington to head the Provincials, & engage the enemy in their own way; but the propriety of it was not seen into until it was too late for execution. After this, many attempts were made to dislodge the enemy from an eminence on the Right but[42] they all proved ineffectual, and fatal to the Officers who by great exertions and good examples endeavoured to accomplish it. — In one of these the General received the Wound of which he died; but previous to it, had several horses killed & disabled under him. — Captains Orme & Morris (his two Aids de Camp, having received wounds which rendered them unable to attend) George Washington remained the sole aid through the day, to the General; he also had one horse killed, and two wounded under him — a ball through his hat — and several through his clothes but escaped unhurt. — Sir Peter Halket (second in Command) being early killed Lieutenant Colonel Burton & Sir Jonathan St. Clair (who had the Rank of Lieutenant Colonel in the Army) being badly wounded — Lieutenant Colonel Gage (afterwards General Gage) having received a contusion — No person knowing in the disordered state things were who the surviving Senior officer was & The Troops by degrees going off in confusion; — without a ray of hope left of further opposition from those that remained; George Washington placed the General in a small covered Cart, which carried some of his most essential equipage, and in the best order he could, with his best Troops (who only continued to be fired at) brought him over the *first* ford of the Monongahela, where they were formed in the best order circumstances would admit on a piece of rising ground; after which, by the Generals order, he rode forward to halt those which had been earlier in the Retreat: Accordingly, after crossing the Monongahela the *second time* and ascending the heights, he found Lieutenant Colonel Gage engaged in this business to whom he delivered the Generals order and then returned to report the situation he found them in — When he was again requested by the General whom he met coming on in his litter with the first halted troops, to proceed (it then being after sundown) to the second division under the command of Colonel Dunbar, to make arrangements for

Life of Washington: The Soldier (Battle of Monongahela) (1854), lithograph by Regnier.
Courtesy of the Library of Congress.

covering the Retreat, and forwarding on provisions & refreshments to the Retreating & wounded Soldiers — To accomplish this, for the 2d division was 40 odd miles in the Rear it took up the whole[43] night & part of the next Morning — which from the weak state in which he was, and the fatigues, and anxiety of the last 24 hours, rendered him in a manner wholly unfit for the execution of the duty he was sent upon when he arrived at Dunbars camp. To the best of his power, however, he discharged it, and remained with the second division till the other joined it. — The shocking[44] scenes which presented themselves in this Nights march are not to be described — The dead — the dying — the groans — lamentations — and crys along the Road of the wounded for help (for those under the latter descriptions endeavoured from the first commencement of the action — or rather confusion to escape to the 2d division) were enough to pierce a heart of adamant. — The gloom & horror of which was not a little encreased by the impervious darkness occasioned by the close shade of thick woods which in places rendered it impossible for the two guides which attended to know when they were in, or out of the track but by groping on the ground with their hands.[45]

Happy was it for him, and the remains of the first division that they left such a quantity of valuable and enticing baggage on the field as to occasion a scramble and contention in the seizure & distribution of it among the enemy for had a pursuit taken place — by passing the defile which we had avoided; and they had got into our Rear, the whole except a few woodsmen, would have fallen victims to the merciless savages. Of about 12 or 13 hundred which were in this action eight or 9 hundred were either killed or wounded, among whom a large proportion of brave and valuable Officers were included[46] — The folly & consequence of opposing compact bodies to the sparse manner of Indian fighting in woods, which had in a manner been predicted, was now so clearly verified that from hence forward another mode obtained in all future operations.

As soon as the two divisions united, the whole retreated towards Fort Cumberland; and at an Incampment near the Great Meadows the brave, but unfortunate General Braddock breathed his last.— He was interred with the honors of War, and as it was left to George Washington to see this performed, & to mark out the spot for the reception of his remains to guard against a savage triumph, if the place should be discovered. They were deposited in the Road over which the Army waggons, &c. passed to hide every trace by which the entombment could be discovered. Thus died a man, whose good & bad qualities were intimately blended. He was brave even to a fault and in regular service would have done honor to his profession—His attachments were warm—his enmities were strong and having no disguise about him, both appeared in full force.— He was generous & disinterested—but plain and blunt in his manner even to rudeness.— After this event, the Troops continued their March for, & soon arrived at Fort Cumberland without molestation; and all except the Provincials immediately resolved to proceed to Philadelphia; by which means the Frontiers of *that* State but *more especially* those of Virginia and Maryland were laid *entirely* open by the *very avenue* which had been prepared.— Of the direful consequences of this measure George Washington, in a visit which he immediately made to Williamsburgh for that purpose brought the Governor & Council of Virginia acquainted—But in vain did they remonstrate against the March of the British Troops to that place to the officer commanding them. They proceeded to augment their own, the command of[47] which under a very enlarged & dignified Commission, to Command *all* the Troops now Raised, or to be Raised in the Colony, was given to him with very extensive powers, and blank Commissions to appoint all

New Officers. About this time also or soon after it the discontents and clamours of the Provincial Officers, and the remonstrance of George Washington in person, to General Shirley, the then Commander in chief of the British Forces in America and through the Governor & Council to the Kings Minister with respect to the degrading situation in which they were placed a new arrangement took place by the Kings order, by which every Provincial Officer was to Rank according to the Command he bore, but to be Junior to those of the same grade in the established Corps. —

As George Washington foresaw, so it happened, the frontiers were continually harrassed — but not having force enough to carry the War to the gates of Du Quesne, he could do no more than distribute the Troops along the Frontiers in Stockaded Forts; more with a view to quiet the fears of the Inhabitants than from any expectation of giving security on so extensive a line to the settlements. During this interval in one of his tours along the frontier posts — he narrowly escaped, according to the account afterwards given by some of our People who were Prisoners with them, and eye witnesses at the time [*illegible*] falling by an Indian party who had waylaid (for another purpose) the communication along which with a small party of horse only he was passing — The road in this place formed a curve and the prey they were in weight for[48] being expected at the reverse part, the Captain of the party had gone across to observe the number & manner of their movement &c. in order that he might make his disposition accordingly leaving orders for the party not to take notice of any passengers the other way till he returned to them — in the meantime in the opposite direction I passed & escaped almost certain destruction for the weather was raining and the few Carbines unfit for use if we had escaped the first fire — This happened near Fort Vass.[49] Never ceasing in the meantime in his attempts, to demonstrate to the Legislature of Virginia—to Lord Loudoun—&c—that the only means of preventing the devastations to which the middle states were exposed, was to remove the cause. But the war by this time raging in another quarter of the Continent all applications were unheeded till the year 1758 when an Expedition against Fort Du Quesne was concerted, and undertaken under the conduct of General Forbes; who tho a brave & good Officer, was so much debilitated by bad health, and so illy supplied with the means to carry on the expedition, that it was November before the Troops got to Loyal hanning 50 or 60 miles short of Du Quesne & even then was on the very point of abandoning the Expedition when some seasonable supplies arriving the Army was formed into three Brigades took up its March and moved forward; The Brigade commanded by George Washington being the leading one.—

Previous to this, and during the time the Army lay at Loyal hanning, a circumstance occurred which involved the life of George Washington in as much jeopardy as it had ever been before or since. The enemy[50] sent out a large detachment to Reconnoitre our Camp, and to ascertain our strength; in consequence of Intelligence that they were within 2 miles of the Camp a party commanded by a Lieutenant Colonel Mercer of the Virginia line (a gallant & good Officer) was sent to dislodge them between whom a severe conflict & hot firing ensued which lasting some time & appearing to approach the Camp it was conceived that our party was yielding the ground upon which George Washington with permission of the General called (per dispatch) for Volunteers and immediately marched at their head to sustain, as was conjectured the retiring troops.— led on by the firing till he came within less than half a mile, & it ceasing, he detached Scouts to investigate the cause & to communicate his approach to his friend Colonel Mercer advancing slowly in the meantime—But it being near dusk and the intelligence not having been fully dissiminated among Colonel Mercers Corps, and they taking us, for the enemy who had retreated approaching in another direction commenced a heavy fire upon the relieving party which drew fire in return in spite of all the exertions of the Officers one of whom & several privates were killed and many wounded before a stop could be put to it. To accomplish which George Washington never was in more imminent danger by being between two fires, knocking up with his sword the presented pieces.[51]

When the Army had got within 12 or 15 miles of the Fort, the enemy dispairing of its defense, blew it up having first embarked their Artillery Stores & Troops—and Retreated by water down the Ohio to their Settlements below[52]—Thus ended that Campaign a little before Christmas in very inclement weather and the last one made during that War by George Washington whose health by this time (as it had been declining for many months before, occasioned by an inveterate disorder in his Bowels) became so precarious as to induce him (having seen quiet restored by this event to the Frontiers of his own Country which was the principal inducement to his taking arms) to resign his Military appointments—The sollicitation of the Troops which he commanded to continue—Their Affectionate farewell address to him, when they found the Situation of his health and other circumstances would not allow it, affected him exceedingly and in grateful sensibility he expressed the warmth of his attachment to them on that, and his inclination to serve them on every other future occasion.—[*end GW note*][53]⟩

He was to have been joined by a Detachment of Independent Regulars from the Southern Colonies, together with some Provincials from North Carolina & Maryland. Without waiting for their arrival he commenced his march in the Month of May. Notwithstanding his precipitate advance, on his ascend-

ing the Laurel-Hill, 50 miles short of his object, he was advised
that a body of French had taken possession & erected a forti-
fication, which they named fort duQuesne. He fell back to a
place known by the appellation of the great meadows, for the
sake of forage & supplies. His force, when joined by Captain
McKay's Regulars, did not amount to 400 men.[54]

These hostilities happened between the subjects of England
& France in America, before those Nations had come to an
open rupture in Europe. In 1755 the British government sent
out to this Country General[55] Braddock, who, with two veteran Regiments, a Detachment of Artillery, several independent Companies of Regulars, & some Corps of Provincials, was
to repel the French from the confines of the English Settlements. Upon a dispute respecting relative rank between the
Regulars & Provincial Officers, Colonel Washington relinquished the command of his Regiment & went as an Aid de
Camp into the family of General Braddock.[56] In this capacity,
at the bloody battle of Monongahela he attended that General,
whose life was gallantly sacrificed in attempting to extricate his
Troops from the fatal ambuscade into which his overweening
confidence had conducted them. Braddock had several horses
killed under him, before he fell himself; and there was not an
officer, whose duty obliged him to be on horseback that day,
excepting Colonel Washington, who was not either killed or
wounded. As soon as [Colonel Washington] had secured their
passage over the ford of the Monongahela & found they were
not pursued; he hastened to concert measures for their farther
security with Colonel Dunbar, who had remained with the
second Division & heavy baggage at some distance in the rear.
To effect this, he travelled, with two guides, all night, through
an almost impervious wilderness[57] notwithstanding the fatigue
he had undergone during the day, and notwithstanding he
had so imperfectly recovered from a severe sickness that he

was obliged in the morning to be supported with cushions on horseback. The public accounts in Europe & America were not parcimonious of praise for the essential services he rendered on so trying an occasion.

The regulation of rank, injurious to the Provincial officers was altered in consequence of repeated applications of Colonel Washington; & the Supreme Authority of Virginia, impressed with a due sense of his Merits, gave him the extensive command of all the Troops raised & to be raised in that Colony.[58]

It would not comport with the intended brevity of this sketch, to mention in detail the places he suggested or the system he pursued for defending the frontier, untill the year 1758, when he commanded the van Brigade of General Forbes's army, in the capture of fort DuQuesne. A similar reason will preclude the description of many personal hazards & atcheivments which happened in the course of his service.

The success of this campaign having restored tranquility on the frontiers of the Middle States and the health of Washington having become extremely debilitated by an inveterate pulmonary complaint, in 1759 he resigned his military appointment.[59] The tender regret of the Virginia Line & the affectionate regard of their Commander might be illustrated by authentic documents.[60]

His health was gradually restored; he married Mrs Custis, a handsome & amiable young widow, possessed of[61] an ample jointure; and settled himself as a planter & farmer on the estate where he now resides in Fairfax County. After some years, he gave up planting tobacco & went altogether into the farming business. Before the war he raised [blank] bushels of wheat, in one year. ⟨GW note: I believe about 7,000 Bushels of Wheat and 10,000 bushels of Indian corn which was more the staple of the farm[62]⟩ Although he has confined his own cultivation to this domestic tract of about 10000[63] acres, yet he possesses excellent lands, in large quantities, in several other Counties. His judgment in the quality of soils, his command of money to avail himself of purchases, and his occasional employment in early life as a Surveyor, gave him opportunities of making advantageous locations, many of which are much improved.

In the interval that took place, from the War between Great Britain & the House of Bourbon which ended in 1763, to the civil war between Great Britain & her Colonies which commenced in 1775, he cultivated the arts of peace. He was constantly a Member of the Assembly, a Magistrate of his County, & a Judge of the Court. He was elected a Delegate to the first Continental Congress in 1774, as well as to that assembled in the year following.[64]

That interval, between the abolition of the Colonial governments, which depended upon Britain & the institution of others independent of it, presents the most curious subject for speculation.[65] The Americans, perhaps, gloried fondly in the fame of their fathers. They delighted in sharing in the battles with Britons & in partaking their triumphs. The most distant nations of the world, which had been summoned by order of arms were lulled into tranquility.[66] The belligerent powers of Europe, exhausted by efforts beyond their strength as it were & faint with loss of blood, had sheathed the murderous steel. It required a course of years & succession of provocations to dissolve those tender yet powerful ties which seemed to be interwoven with the very fibres of our hearts.[67]

Notwithstanding the little obscure intervals when the face of Britain was covered with a cloud or her arm shortened that it could not save, [the colonies were] sunned by her eye & fostered by her hand. Long had the mother-country enjoyed the exclusive advantage of our trade. We acquiesced & were becoming daily more profitable to her. The vine, planted in Heathen lands had become prolific in fruit as luxuriant in

growth. But the fruit was not yet ripe. The British administration would not wait for the vintage which must have fallen into
their lap. They gave orders for stripping the vines. Gathered by
premature avulsion, & trodden in the press of ministerial wrath
by mercenary troops, the clusters produced blood for wine.[68]

In these alarming circumstances no alternative was submitted to their decision. After blood had been shed by the British,
it was commonly said in allusion to an invasion that The Rubi-
con was passed. Necessity dictated that the best means should
be adopted for defence: Prudence that men, who possessed
the public confidence, should be chosen to conduct the operations. There was one man, who, from his local situation in
the centre of the Colonies; from his private character without
a stain, from his ample property which must of consequence
be risqued upon the issue of the contest, from his complicated abilities which were confessedly of the most useful kind,
from the mature time of life at which he had arrived when the
mental as well as corporeal faculties are thought to be in the
highest state of perfection and from the established reputation
he had acquired by his military services in a former war, was
looked upon as without the least measure of art or intrigue
as designated by Heaven for their leader. As no cabal existed,
no canvassing happened: But It was not difficult to know the
general wish; and Congress was never more truly the organ of
the People, than on the [*blank*] day of June 1775, in announcing the appointment of Mr Washington to be Commander in
Chief of the forces of the United Colonies.[69] He, comprehend-
ing clearly the magnitude of the trust & the importance of
its functions,[70] unelated with the splendid power of command,
after several days anxious deliberation, upon conviction of its
thus being his indispensable duty, with marks of unfeigned diffidence, accepted the Charge & thus, from his place,[71] informed
Congress: "Mr President [*blank.*]"[72]

General Washington, having now entered of upon a new walk of life, A more ample range for the display of whatever talents he possessed was laid open before him. The field almost unbounded as it appeared, was however hedged with darkness & difficulty on every side. The war was considered through no milder medium than that of violated majesty & denominated by no softer terms than that of a wanton rebellion, by the Publications of the British Commander in Chief at Boston; as well as in the Proclamations of his Royal Master at St James. Pains & penalties of a sanguinary nature were denounced against[73] the authors & abettors of it. Want of success must not only have consigned the neck of the American General as the Arch Rebel, to the block, but his name, to infamy. Thus was he exalted to an Awful pre-eminence, where, in the view of sober reason, more than the equal chances were to be calculated upon the failure of our defence. But, by how much the more perilous than any other, by so much the less enviable, was the elevated post in which he was placed, in which would be wanted all the vigour, all the wisdom & all the fortitude of a mind prepared for events. Every circumstance conspired with his character to command respect & extinguish rivalship. The cares that would of course devolve upon him, in the conduct of such a war, where scarcly one article for annoyance or defence had been previously provided, must be most intolerable.[74] It was a saying among his friends, in conversation, that in a complicated command more depended upon choosing proper persons to conduct the different departments, than in performing one's own particular part with ability.[75] The care of fighting [was] much less than that of feeding an army.[76] Nor could he have[77] supported himself beneath the presure, at any other period of life, notwithstanding the unbroken firmness of constitution & the unshaken resolution of soul with which nature seemed to have formed him to meet the shocks of adversity. In the good wishes & ready assistances of his countrymen, whether as public bodies or private citizens, the General, however, found for supplying many exigencies, a resourse whose value could not be easily appreciated.[78] Congress, who pledged their lives & properties, of right trusting to his capacity, integrity & patriotism, only instructed him to go on [*blank*] in cause of God & their country, [and] soon appointed [*blank*.][79]

Immediately after these appointments, General Washington escorted by a Troop of Volunteer Dragoons in company with General Lee & several other officers departed from Philadelphia for Cambridge. He travelled by as great journeys as the civilities he was obliged to receive & the arrangements he was under the necessity of making on the road, would admit. Retarded by some casualities & dissuaded from crossing the bay from Elizabeth Town to New York lest the ships in the harbour should attempt to seize his person, he arrived there the 24th of June & was received by the new formed military Corps & all the Citizens (except the professed adherents to the British Government) with demonstrations of joy. The Provincial Congress of that Colony, then assembled in the city of New York, through the mouth of their President, hastened to inform the Commander in Chief: "That, at a time when the most loyal of his Majesty's Subjects, from a regard to the Laws & the Constitution by which he sat on[80] the throne, felt themselves reduced to the unhappy necessity of taking up arms to defend their dearest rights & privileges; and while they deplored the calamities of a divided empire, they rejoiced in the appointment of a gentleman, from whose abilities & virtues they were taught to expect both security & peace: that, moreover, confiding in him & the worthy Generals immediately under his command, they had the most flattering hopes of success in the glorious struggle for American liberty; and the fullest assurances that whensoever the important contest should result in that fond-

est wish of each American Soul, an accomodation with the
mother Country, he would cheerfully resign the important de-
posit committed to his hands, and resume the character of
the Worthiest Citizen." The General replied, "Gentlemen, at
[*blank.*] [81]

At that place he had an interview with Major General
Schuyler, a man of great understanding & personal activity,
but feeble in health & destitute of those popular talents which
are peculiarly necessary in a new army, now second in rank &
destined to a seperate department at the Northward. He gave
him orders in writing to take the command of that Department
to carry into effect such designs of the Continental Congress
as fell within his province (with which object, a transcript of
Instructions from that Body to the General in Chief Command) to possess & fit for defence the Posts recommended
by [82] the Provincial Convention; to take charge of the Stores
which were or ought to have been removed from the city of
New York; to keep a watchful eye on Governor Tryon, so as
to frustrate any schemes inimical to the common cause which
he might meditate, and to receive the directions of Congress,
in case there should appear to be a necessity for arresting the
Governor; to watch the conduct of Colonel Guy Johnson, the
Indian agent, for the purpose of obviating the effects of his influence in rendering the Savages hostile; to obtain information
of the temper of the Indians & Canadians that a proper kind of
treatment towards them might be adopted; to supply the Posts
on lake Champlain with provisions & ammunition, on the best
terms so as "to prevent our good cause from sinking under a
heavy load of expence"; to remit monthly Returns of troops &
stores, together with more frequent advices of every thing that
might be deemed important; and lastly to regulate all matters,
not particularly pointed out, according to his own good sense,
as it was not wished to circumscribe him within narrow limits.

The General, having spent two days in making the necessary arrangements, & having his reports to Congress with an earnest request & solicitation that powder might be speedily supplied; proceeded on his[83] journey, accompanied for some distance by all the Corps of the City.[84]

It is the less necessary to particularize, his transactions in the course of the late war, because the impression which he made is yet fresh in every mind. But it is hoped Posterity will be taught, in what manner he transformed an undisciplined body of Peasantry into a regular army of Soldiers. Commentaries on his Campaigns would be at once highly interesting & instructive to them. The conduct of the first onset, in obliging the British Troops to abandon Boston by a bloodless victory, will merit to be minutely related. But a volume would hardly contain the mortifications he experienced & the hazards to which he was exposed in 1776 & 1777, in contending against the prowess of Britain, with an inadequate force. His good destiny & consummate prudence prevented want of success from producing, want of confidence, on the part of the Public, which is apt to lead to the adoption of pernicious counsels, through the levity of the People or the ambition of their Demagogues. Shortly after this period sprang up the only Cabal, that ever existed during his public life, to rob him of his reputation & command.[85] It proved as impotent in effect, as it was audacious in contemplation. In the three succeeding years the germe of discipline insensibly unfolded; and the resources of America having been called into co-operation with the land & naval armies of France produced[86] the glorious conclusion of the campaign in 1781. From this time the gloom began to disappear from our political horizon, and the affairs of the Union proceeded in a meliorating train, untill an advantageous peace was most ably negotiated by our Ambassadors in Europe, in 1783.[87]

Colonel David Humphreys Presenting to Congress Colors Captured at Yorktown (ca. 1840), painting by unknown artist. Courtesy of the New Haven Colony Historical Society.

One of the most amiable & useful services which he rendered to the U.S., has not, to my knowledge been noticed by any writer: I mean the wise care he bestowed on & the wonderful agency he had in, eradicating the prejudices against each, which existed in an eminent degree between the Inhabitants of the various American Colonies before the Revolution. It was naturally the policy of the Mother Country, to prevent a coalition in sentiment & actions; and nothing is more likely to produce this situation to make the one think unfavorably or [*illegible*] of each other. The people of one half of the Continent, knew little or nothing of the real character of those in another; and the information which was generally given them was respecting the foibles or singularities, rather than the virtues and merits of those who were placed at a distance from them. There was little intercourse to enable discerning & candid men to form just ideas. At that time, So great was the confidence of the British Government, & even its Partizans among ourselves, of the impossibility of reconciling the Colonists so as to act cordially together against the [88] Troops of Great Britain, a belief was entertained this spirit of disunion would so facilitate their operations that they had little more to do than to avail themselves of that circumstance for making a speedy & almost bloodless conquest. I have frequently been present, when it was asserted by the Royalists, in the most positive terms, that the Eastern Colonies, could expect no concurrence or aid from the Southern; nor they in turn any from the others; and that oil & water would not incorporate with more difficulty, that military forces which were levying in what was then first denominated the Union. But so effectually did General Washington recommend, by his example & caution, that harmony on which the success of an army so essentially depends, that perhaps better order & more cordiality never existed than in the American Camp. Men of good sense & good dispositions accustomed themselves to consider & treat those of the same character, wheresoever born or however educated, as worthy of their sincere friendship. Nor did the happy effects of this amicable acquaintance terminate here. They carried the same sensations & impressions into private life at the conclusion of the war.[89] Men [were] coming together in Congress & [they] tended also to obtain new ideas.[90]

No person, who had not the advantage of being present when General Washington received the intelligence of peace & who did not accompany him to his domestic retirement, can describe the relief which that joyful event brought to his labouring mind, or the satisfaction with which he withdrew to the shades of private life. From his Triumphant Entry into New York, upon the evacuation of that city by the British Army, to his arrival at Mount Vernon, after the resignation of his commission to Congress, festive crowds impeded his passage through all the populous towns, the devotion of a whole people pursued him with prayers to Heaven for blessings on his head, while their gratitude sought the most expressive language of manifesting itself to him, as their common father & benefactor. When he became a citizen, he had the uncommon felicity to find that his native State was among the most zealous in doing justice to his merits, & that stronger demonstrations of affectionate esteem (if possible) were given by the[91] citizens in his neighbourhood, than by any other description of men on the Continent.[92] ⟨*GW note:* Whether it be necessary to mention that my time & Services were given to the public without compensation, and that every direct and indirect attempt afterwards, to reward them (as appeared by the Letter of G. Mifflin—and the vote of 50 shares in each of the Navigations of Potomack & James River by the State of Virginia who knew that I would refuse anything that should carry with it the appearance of reward—you can best judge.— [93]⟩ But he has constantly declined accepting of any compensation for his services, or provision for the augmented expenses which have been incurred in consequence of his public employment, although proposals have been made in the most delicate manner, particularly by the States of Virginia & Pennsylvania.[94]

When he first came home from the army, he found his affairs, which had formerly been well arranged, in great disorder. In the war Taxes had been high, articles necessary to be purchased for a family dear, & crops in a considerable degree unprofitable. In addition to these causes of embarrassment, large sums of money which had been placed at interest, during his absence were paid to his Agent in a depreciated paper currency. Insomuch that his estate at his return was £10,000 sterling worse, than when he left it. At this time the expences of his house had also encreased, by reason of the multitude of company which resorted thither; to an exorbitant sum. His house was all this winter & spring filled with gentlemen, his offices with their servants, & his stables with their horses. No sooner had one party quitted it, than another arrived. (These visits were so many tributes of homage or friendship, which official characters & intimate acquaintances could not well dispense with themselves for not paying. Among the former were the President of Congress, the Governor of the State, the Ambassador of France, the Baron Steuben late Inspector General of the army & many others who had just then divested themselves of the military character). In this situation,[95] it was difficult for him to command enough of his own time, for carrying on his different correspondences. This circumstance he noticed in his private letters, particularly in that which he wrote in answer to one from Governor Jefferson, wherein that gentleman suggested whether it would not be compatible with General Washington's determination of remaining the rest of his days in retirement, for him to Superintend the opening of the navigation of the great Rivers in Virginia.[96]

The virtuous simplicity which distinguishes the private life of General Washington, though less known than the dazzling splendour of his military atcheivments, is not less edifying in example & ought not to be less interesting to his countrymen. The conspicuous character he has acted on the Theatre of human affairs, the dignity with which he sustained his part amidst difficulties of the most discouraging nature, & the Glory of having arrived through them at the hour of triumph, have made many official & literary persons, on both sides of the Ocean, ambitious of a correspondence with him. These correspondencies unavoidably engross a great portion of his time; and the communications contained in them, combined with the numerous periodical Publications & News Papers which he peruses, render him, as it were, the focus of political Intelligence for the New World. Nor are his conversations with well-informed men, less conducive to bring him acquainted with the various events which happen, in different countries of the globe. Every foreigner, of distinction, who visits America, makes it a point to see him.[97] Members of Congress & other dignified Personages do not pass his house without calling to pay their respects. As another source of information it may be mentioned, that many literary productions are sent to him annually by their Authors in Europe; & that there is scarcely one work written in America on any art, science, or subject which does not seek his protection, or which is not offered to him as a token of gratitude. Mechanical inventions are frequently submitted for his approbation & natural curiosities presented for his investigation. But the multiplicity of epistolary applications, often on the remains of some business which happened when he was Commander in Chief, sometimes on subjects foreign to his situation, frivolous in their nature, & intended merely to gratify the vanity of the writers by drawing answers from him, is truly distressing & almost incredible. His benignity in answering perhaps encreases the number. Did he not husband every moment to the best advantage, it would not be in his power to notice the vast variety of objects that claim his attention. Here a minuter description of his domestic life may be expected.

To apply a short life to the most useful purposes, he lives, as he ever has done, in the unvarying habits of regularity,[98] temperance, & industry. He rises, in winter as well as summer, at the dawn of day; and generally reads or writes some time before breakfast. He breakfasts about 7 O'Clock on three small Indian Hoe-cakes, & as many dishes of tea. He rides immediately to his different farms & remains with his labourers untill a little past two O'Clock, when he returns & dresses. At three he dines, commonly on a single dish, and drinks from half a pint to a pint of Madeira wine. This, with one small glass of punch, a draught of beer, and two dishes of tea (which he takes half an hour before sun-set) constitutes his whole sustenance, untill the next day. Whether there be company or not, the table is always prepared by its elegance & exuberance for their reception; and the General remains at it for an hour after dinner, in familiar conversation & convivial hilarity.[99] He is more chearful than he was in the army. Notwithstanding his temper is rather of a serious cast & his countenance commonly carries the impression of thoughtfulness; he perfectly relishes a pleasant story, an unaffected sally of wit, or a burlesque description which surprises by its suddenness & incongruity with the ordinary appearance of the same object. After the sociable relaxation, he applies himself[100] to business, & about 9 O'Clock retires to rest. This the rotine, & this the hour he observes, when no one but his family is present; at other times,

he attends politely upon his company untill they wish to with-
draw. Though he has no offspring, his actual family consists of
eight persons: it is seldom alone.* He keeps a pack of hounds,
& in the season indulges himself with hunting once in a week,
at which diversion the gentlemen of Alexandria often assist.[102]
⟨*GW note:* Once a week is his fixed hunts tho sometimes he
goes oftener.[103]⟩

Agriculture is the favorite employment of General Washington, in which he wishes to pass the remainder of his days. To
acquire practical knowledge, he corresponds with Mr Arthur
Young who has written so sensibly on the subject; ⟨*GW note:*
And many others in this Country[104]⟩ as also with many agricultural gentlemen in this Country; and as improvement is known
to be his passion, he receives envoys of rare seeds & results
of new projects, from every quarter. He also makes copious
Notes in writing relative to his own experiments the state of
the seasons, nature of soils, effect of different kinds of manure
& everything that can throw light on the farming business.
⟨*GW note:* remarking the state of the Weather—nature of the
Soil &c. The information given in these sheets—tho related
from Memory, It is I believe to be depended upon.— It is
hastily and incorrectly related—but not so much for these reasons, as some others, it is earnestly requested that after Colonel
Humphreys has extracted What he shall judge necessary, and
given it in his own language, that the *whole* of what Is here
contained may be returned to George Washington, or com-

---

*[*Humphreys' note:*] The family of General Washington, in addition to
the General & his Lady, consists of Major George Washington (nephew
to the General & late Aid de Camp to the Marquis de la Fayette) with
his wife who is a neice to the General's Lady—Colonel Humphreys, formerly Aid de Camp to the General—Mr Lear, a gentleman of liberal
education from New England, private Secretary to the General—and two
Grand-Children of Mrs Washington.[101]

General George Washington and His Family, engraving by George E. Perine. Courtesy of the Library of Congress.

mitted to the flames. — some of the enumerations are trifling; and perhaps more important circumstances omitted; — but just as they occurred to the memory, they were committed. If there are any grains among them Colonel Humphreys can easily seperate them from the chaff.[105]) Every week, On Saturday in the afternoon, reports are made by all his Overseers & registered in books kept for the purpose; so that at the end of the year, the quantity of labour & produce may be accurately known.[106] Order & economy are established in all the Departments within & without doors. His lands are enclosed in lots of equal dimensions & crops are assigned to each for many years. Every thing is undertaken on a great scale,[107] but with a view to introduce or augment the culture of such articles, as he conceives will become most beneficial in their consequence to the country. In the mean time, the Public may rest persuaded that he manufactures woolen & linen cloths in quantities nearly or quite sufficient, for the use of his numerous household.[108] He has, this year, raised 200 lambs, sowed 27 bushels of flaxseed & planted more than 700 bushels of potatoes.[109]

Mount Vernon, the celebrated seat of General Washington, is pleasantly situated on the Virginian bank of the river Potowmac, where it is nearly 2 miles wide & about 280 from the sea. Mount Vernon is 9 miles below the flourishing Town of Alexandria & 4 above the beautiful Situation of the late Honorable Colonel George Fairfax, called Bellevoir. The area of the Mount, is 200 feet above the surface of the water, and, after furnishing a lawn of 5 acres in front & about the same in rear of the buildings, falls off rather abruptly on those two quarters. On the north-end it subsides gradually into extensive pasture grounds; while on the south it slopes more steeply in a shorter distance, and terminates with the coach-house, stables, vineyard & nurseries. On either wing is a dense & opaque grove of different flowering forest trees. Parellel with them, on the land-side, are two spacious gardens, into which one is led by two serpentine gravel-walks, planted with weeping willows & umbrageous shrubs. The Mansion House itself, though much embellished by yet not perfectly satisfactory to the chaste taste of the present Possessor, appears venerable & convenient. The superb banquetting room has been finished since he returned home from the army. A lofty Portico, 96 feet in length, supported by eight pillars, has a pleasing effect when viewed from [110] the water; and the *tout ensemble*, of the green-house, school-house, offices & servants-halls when seen from the country-side, bears a resemblance to a rural village: especially as the lands in that site are laid out somewhat according to the form of English gardens, in meadows & grass-grounds, ornamented with little copses, circular clumps, & single trees.[111] [O]n the opposite side of a little creek to the Northward, an extensive plain, exhibiting cornfields & cattle grazing, affords in summer a luxurus landscape to the eye; While the cultivation declivities, intermingle with woodlands on the Maryland shore concludes the prospect; While to blended verdure of woodlands & cultivated declivities on the Maryland shore variegates the prospect on another side in a charming manner.[112] A small Park on the margin of the river, where the English fallow-deer & the American wild-deer are seen through the thickets, alternately with the vessels as they are sailing along, adds a romantic & picturesque appearance to the whole scenery. Such are the philosophic shades, to which the late Commander in Chief of the American armies has retired, from the tumultuous scenes of a busy world.[113]

*　　*　　*

As soon as the Convention had finished their business the General returned to Mount Vernon. This summer had been remarkably dry there & his crops so much injured, that he was obliged to buy nearly 1000 barrels of corn for the support of his people. Notwithstanding his experiments to introduce more advantageous modes of cultivation had been thus rendered unsuccessful, he still persisted in practicing them. Believing that the amelioration of agriculture was the best resource of prosperity for this country, his attention was almost wholly occupied by projects of this kind & he scarcly failed a single day, to ride to his different plantations. Even on the days when he hunted, he contrived to visit the labourers at some of his farms. His passion [114] for hunting, which had been rather keen, in his youthful days, was now so far abated as to be subordinate to almost every ordinary avocation. After this season it became altogether extinct; though he still kept a pack of hounds the succeeding year, he went not once to the chace. [115]

In November Colonel Humphreys came to reside at Mount Vernon in consequence of repeated invitations: [116] One of which was conceived in these terms, —. As the people were now to determine whether they would accept or reject the proposed form of government, the proceedings in the several States must of course be very interesting. The General sent regularly twice in a week to the Post Office in Alexandria, from whence he never failed to receive letters & News-Papers from many parts of the U.S. In the compass of the fall & winter, the States of Delaware, Pennsylvania, Georgia, [117] Jersey, Connecticut, & Massachusetts, that order of succession in which they are named adopted the government. Sharp contests in the Conventions of Pennsylvania & Massachusetts took place. [118] In the latter, the Adherents to the new Constitution, commonly denominated federalists, were accused by the Antifederalists of unfairness in having precipitated the State into an accession by surprize, while a majority of the freemen were opposed to the measure. The early decision of Pennsylvania probably had some influence on the conduct of the other States; where their Convention[s] were moved to a later day. But The Accu-

Washington at Mount Vernon, engraving by McNevin and J. Rogers. Courtesy of the Library of Congress.

sation was in a degree refuted by the appointment of persons
who were friendly to the system for Senators & Representa-
tives in Congress, as well as for Electors of President & Vice
President. In the interim much opposition was expected in
North Carolina, Virginia, New York & Rhode Island. While
the Gazettes teemed with compositions on the one part calculated to impress the Citizens with an opinion[119] of their
dangerous situation & the consequent necessity of embracing
the Constitution; some Gazettes on the other part abounded
with peices designed to alarm their fears in regard to the pernicious effects of the Constitution & to dissuade them from
consenting that it should be carried into execution. Besides
these news-paper publications, some more elaborate treatises
on both sides of the question were printed. Among those in
opposition to the[120] government, that under the signature of a
federal Farmer was thought to be the best written; & among
those in favor of it, The Federalist was incontestably a performance of superior merit.[121] While things remained in this
situation, General Washington took no part publicly or pri-
vately in the dispute. Extracts from one or two of his letters in
answer to those of some of his correspondents, & expressive of
his individual idea of the inexpediency of assembling another
federal Convention, were, indeed, made public, without his
knowledge & contrary to his wishes.[122] Notwithstanding he
conceived the welfare of his country depended greatly upon
the acceptance of the proposed Constitution; yet the frequent
paragraphs in the news-papers holding forth the necessity of
his being appointed President of the U.S., & the intimations
of many of his friends, in Europe & America, to the same
effect, precluded him from that activity, which he might otherwise have thought himself at liberty to use on so important
an occasion.[123] He was, however, not the less anxious to know
the progress of the business. He sent regularly twice in every

week to the Post office in Alexandria, whence he failed not to
receive letters, & news-papers, from most parts of the Union.
Members of Congress, foreigners, other strangers, & visiting
friends often brought additional & more minute intelligence.
Even in the domestic circle, when none but the family were [124]
present, news & politics were at this time more frequent topics
of conversation than any other. But nothing directly or indi-
rectly was ever mentioned in the family to or by the General,
which alluded to his appointment to the Presidency, during
that whole winter & spring. To some other persons who attempted to extract from him some sentiment on the subject, he
replied drily, "That it was always time enough for him to give
an answer when any event happened which made an option indispensable; but that he hoped & trusted the event suggested
would never occur." —

About the middle of July General Washington went to meet
the Directors of the Potowmac Company at the Shenadoah
falls; [125] When having found the works at the different places
well advanced & having put the accomplishment of the undertaking in a good train of execution, he returned by a route
which enabled him to visit his brother & freinds in Berk-
ley. The week after his return, he had engaged to go with
Mrs Washington & pay their dutiful respects to his mother at
Fredericksburg. [126] In a Baltimore paper which arrived by the
mail three days before his departure, he observed a paragraph,
announcing that the Citizens of that town had sent the miniature Ship federalist (the same made use of as one of the pag-
eants at the late rejoicing for the adoption of the Constitution
in that State) as a present to him: & by the same mail a letter
came to Mount Vernon, directed to Captain Barney, who had
the charge of bringing round the little ship. The next [127] morning, after breakfast, when the rest of the company had all left
the room, he took an occasion of speaking to Colonel Hum-

phreys in this manner.[128] "I perceive by the Baltimore Paper
that the Citizens are sending the ship, Federalist, which they
made use of in their late procession, as a present to me: & for
which I am very sorry, I am afraid it is intended to hold up some
kind of an opinion respecting my being employed in the federal
government, in case I should accept their present." Colonel
Humphreys said "That He had observed the same article, &
that he rather believed it to be intended only as a mark of respect, & without being meant as a scheme for drawing any
conclusion with regard to the General's future conduct—He
imagined, however, it could not but be obvious to the General
that the People of the Continent had turned their eyes upon
him as the person, whom they wished to be President, & that
the time would ere long approach when he would be under the
necessity of making a decision.["] General Washington returned "that indeed it was a subject, which could not have
escaped his attention, since he [had] seen it mentioned in the
public Papers, & since had received private letters respecting
it, & even applications for office under the new government—
that although he could not avoid flattering himself[129] that he
should not be appointed; yet that these things had been very
distressing to him & preyed exceedingly upon his mind.["]—
Colonel Humphreys replied, "He thought from the best information public & confidential, which he could obtain, that
there was the highest probability, amounting nearly to a cer-
tainty, that the appointment would take place; that his decided
opinion, was formerly, when the States appeared much less
unanimous than at present, that it would be the General's indispensable duty to accept, but that acquiescence in the Constitution on the part of all the States might perhaps, make a refusal in some degree warrantable."— The General answered—
"that his resolution was made up to refuse the apointment, in
case it should be offered, unless much stronger reasons should

be presented than had ever occured to him for deviating from his original determination of passing his life in retirement, at present he wished to fall upon some expedient to be freed from the embarrassment, which was likely to happen on the arrival of the Federalist." — Colonel Humphreys told the General, that he ["]apprehended it would be most consistent with his prudence to suspend his final determination, on the great question, untill the [130] circumstances should require a definitive answer, and especially so long as any new lights might be afforded for making his conclusions upon the clearest, & safest & best grounds possible. As to the matter of the ship, an acceptance would probably be necessary; and as he was to go from home in two days, in case it should arrive in his absence, no answer would be required from which any consequence could be deduced." It was then observed by the General "that it was likely a letter would be sent with the vessel, to which he should be under the necessity of writing an answer." The ship arrived next day with a letter from the Proprietors, in reply to which the General wrote one, in such prudent terms, as, notwithstanding its publication, was not attended with any of the ill consequences, which he had apprehended. — [131]

[Washington feared] That after having made known his intentions of remaining in private life, he should cirtainly be reproached with the most glaring inconsistency for having departed from those declarations: That he must also incur the imputation of acting from motives of ambition: and therefore it appeared to him that by accepting the appointment he should injure the interests of the new government, rather than lend any aid towards a quiet acquiescence in it. On the contrary an idea had prevailed in his [132] mind, that, in case of his election, his best way of contributing towards the accomplishment of the government, would be to decline the Office, and at the same time to give his reasons at large for his conduct, attended by all the arguments that might fairly be adduced in favor of this Constitution. He conceived the disinterestedness of this proceeding would be clear in the view of all unprejudiced persons, that his refusal would add a greater weight to his sentiments, than his acceptance. For although his friends who knew him well & perhaps some others, would[133] do justice to the rectitude of his intentions in case he should accept that office in question; yet he had not a right to expect such candour from mankind in general. He added, the more he had thought upon the matter, (and he had thought much upon it) the more he was inclined to believe his acceptance would be improper for himself, & perhaps not profitable for the Public—He hoped, however, that something in the intermediate time might turn up, which should prevent his election & thus superside the necessity of any decision on his own part—He concluded, that he would most willingly take means to prevent the choice, if it could be done without involving him in censures for having been actuated by a strange kind of vanity, in supposing he should be chosen President, when in fact it might be a very doubtful case,: for it was not to be supposed that any Electors who were opposed to the Constitution would vote for him.[134]

[Washington said, "]A part of the awkwardness of the circumstances is, one cannot undertake to say or do anything on such a subject, before the event happens, in case it does happen—& then it is too late to obtain the advice of such friends as one would wish to consult. God knows that I have but one wish myself, which is to live & die on my own plantation. It is said that every man has his portion of ambition. I may have mine I suppose as well as the rest; but if I know my own heart, my ambition would not lead me into public life; my only ambition is to do my duty in this world as well as I am capable of performing it, & to merit the good opinion of all good men.

I am not seeking for a compliment, when I tell you sincerely, that I think there are a great many men in the U.S. much fitter for the office than I am. My life has been a very busy one, I have had but little leisure to read of late years, and even if I had been favored with more leisure, my memory is so bad I can get little advantage from reading. I cannot indeed pretend to be so well acquainted with civil matters, as I was with military affairs. If there was any subject with which I could assume to have some acquaintance it was with the latter.["][135]

During the absence of George Washington, Colonel Robert Harrison, then Chief Justice of Maryland, formerly the Secretary & always the friend of the General, came to visit him.[136] A good deal of conversation happened between that Gentleman & Colonel Humphreys on the subject of the General's election as President & the conduct most proper to be observed by him in consequence of it. Colonel Harrison was clearly of opinion it would be his duty to accept; because his refusal would give such a shock to the friends of the government, & such an advantage to its opponents, that it might possibly produce its entire subversion. He mentioned it had been a common saying with the Antifederalists that their arguments would have appeared with much superior force & that their numbers would have been much greater, if General Washington had been on the other side of the question. he mentioned further, it was believed by many, that the members of the federal Convention, in consequence of the discordant interests of their States, would not have been brought to unite in any plan of government, had it not be[en] for the presence of the General; & that now it was believed his aid would not be less necessary than on any former occasion. Shortly after General Washington's return from Fredericksburg, in the course of a conversation chiefly on politics, the substances of these observations was faithfully reported to him as coming from his friend, & gave rise to the following conversation:[137]

[Humphreys said, "]If the government cannot be carried into effect without you—two things ought principally, in my judgment, to be regarded, when you are making up your mind on that question, which will certainly be referred to your solution: first whether the government may be carried into execution as well without your assistance as with it? & second, what the impartial world, particularly posterity, will believe to have been your motives for a refusal, in case any disagreeable consequences shall have followed from it? My opinion has been formerly, as you know, that no possible circumstances could make it expedient, or perhaps justifiable after your pointed declarations, to the contrary, to come again into public life. But I must avow, that in searching for arguments to justify you in declining the appointment; I have been rather led to & confirmed in an opposite opinion. Perhaps it will be found that the very existence of the government will be much endangered, if the person placed at the Head of it should not possess the entire confidence of both its friends & adversaries. Whoever the President should be, he might expect to meet with some obloquy from its adversaries, though I think you will be as little obnoxious to it as any other. From all the treatment you have ever experienced from the people of this Continent you have a right to believe, that they entertain a good opinion of your abilities—That they entertain a superlatively high opinion of your prudence, integrity & disinterestedness[138] is true & is of the first consequence. You ought, at sometimes, Sir, to look upon the bright side of the picture; and not always to be pondering the objects you find on the Reverse. Nothing but clear common sense & good intentions, in our circumstances, will be necessary for conducting the affairs of the Commonwealth. If the practice of economy, industry & justice can be made prevalent, we cannot fail to become a great & a happy people. We have more advantages for becoming such than any nation on the earth. We only want that the public mind should receive a right biass, at our first beginning to act as a nation. You can do much towards giving that biass, and you will be assisted by the ablest & best men on the Continent. The undertaking to make your country happy, which is now to be entered upon; is not so arduous as that of making it independent, which has already been atchieved—but it is a more pleasing employment, &, if happily executed, will be productive of more true glory. If you shall be instrumental in carrying this government into operation, and in obtaining such modifications as shall quiet the alarms which have be[en] ex[c]ited by certain parts of it in the minds of some well affected citizens, you will do a more essential service to your country, than any other human character will ever have it in his power to perform. If, after having seen your country placed in a situation, capable of enjoying all the public felicity which is incident to the lot of humanity, you shall be at liberty to retire again to domestic life; you may congratulate yourself upon having been at last the most fortunate, the most favored, of mortals.["] [139]

General Washington—the latter part of November having received some dispatches, sent for Colonel Humphreys into his Study, & said to him: "I have just received letters. As the time approaches in which it seems to be thought that the affair, on which we have several times conversed, will happen, I think I feel very much like a man who is condemned to death does when the time of his execution draws nigh—["] [140]

In [the] second conversation [the] General said—He forsaw the nomination of persons to offices would [141] be attended with much ill will & little satisfaction on the part of the Candidates. ["]For, as there would be many competitors for every appointment, only one could be gratified, & all the rest must be displeased, because there are few men who do not really consider their own pretensions, as good at least as those of their rivals. A President cannot know personally the character of Candidates, & is therefore liable to deception: besides it is frequently the

interest of those to whom he is obliged to recur for information, to give him wrong advices. It will consequently be almost
impossible to do right, even with the best intentions: it will be
quite impracticable to avoid giving umbrage & experiencing
unjust imputations. However, in case, I should be in a manner
obliged to accept the Office, I know that merit only ought to
be regarded, & I will endeavour faithfully & disinterestedly to
have men of that discreption, imployed, & selected in as equal
proportions as may be from the different parts of the Continent. I am sensible the Vice President & Senate might do
much towards forwarding or retarding the execution of those
measures; but there is reason to believe the greater number
will be well affected to the government & heartily disposed
to promote the interests of the Union.[142] Some efforts seem to
have been made for drawing a sentiment from me, respecting
the Person I would wish to see chosen for Vice President. so
far am I, however, from desiring to [143] interfere in that matter,
that, in case of my being in office, declare I shall be very well
satisfied with any man who will concur in promoting the public good; even if [*blank*] (naming a man whom he considered
always as a private enemy) were to be chosen, it should not be
my fault if we did not live upon perfectly good terms.—["] [144]
After pausing a moment, he added, ["]but, if my appointment
& acceptance be inevitable, I fear I must bid adieu to happiness, for I see nothing, but clouds & darkness before me: and
I call God to witness that the day which shall carry me again
into public life, will be a more distressing one than any I have
ever yet known"— [145]

*　　*　　*

It was a great advantage to General Washington, in forming
an army composed of men who were on a footing of perfect equality, to have been distinguished for unusual dignity in
his figure, appearance & manners. If many estimable qualities
be connected with that dignified presence which thus con-

ciliates esteem and imposes respect; subordination is always
established with the less difficulty. Such was the case with the
American Commander in Chief & so peculiarly did he seem
fitted for command that no one even in his own mind disputed
the right to the first place. He inherited from Nature a strong
constitution and uncommon force of nerves. Tho' his life had
been endangered by a pulmonic disorder which he contracted
from fatigues in youth; yet by time, temperance & a voyage to
one of the West India Islands he recovered his health & became remarkably robust. No person in the army was capable of
enduring the excess of heat, cold, watching & hardship better
than himself. In the report of his Mission to the western frontiers in his early age, he demonstrated that he possessed good
sense and discriminating judgment in an eminent degree. To
these he joined a purity of intention, which Slander itself has
never attempted to stain. It has been observed in some well-
written dissertations on his character, that his talents were
rather solid[146] than brilliant. It is certain that he never affected
a shining reputation. It is also certain that Heaven had destined him by endowments of different kinds, which are but
rarely bestowed on mortals, to be indeed a great man. Of what
kinds they were, it is not now my purpose or here the place
to discuss. Some have taken a pleasure in exalting & others
in depressing his character for mental abilities & accomplishments. Those who pretended that every thing published in his
name was written by himself and those who desire to have it
believed that he was incapable of being the author of many
of those interesting* compositions, were equally erroneous in
their opinions.

*[*Humphreys' note:*] By intelligence recently received from America it appears that his farewell Addresses on retiring from the Army & declining
to be re-elected President, together with several other interesting compositions are to be collected & published in an elegant manner.[147]

The American, English, French & other Gazettes have announced that General Washington had left behind him a Manuscript History of the American Revolution composed by himself. This article is entirely destitute of truth. He was, however, careful to preserve copies of every order, letter or written document which was dispatched by him or in his name during the whole course of the Revolutionary war. These important papers, before the conclusion of that war, were fairly transcribed into more than thirty volumes in folio, distributed under seperate heads, such as military orders & letters, correspondence with Congress, Chiefs of Departments, Governors of[148] States, Municipal Bodies, Persons in foreign Countries & private Citizens in the United States. For the purpose of shewing what was his opinion on the subject of writing the Commentaries or Memoirs of his Campaigns, a letter (which is now in America) from him to the Author of this work, will probably hereafter be published.[149]

Few men have ever thought with more justice, and consequently few men have ever had clearer ideas or expressed them with more precision than General Washington. At the same time, he knew how, better than any other man, to avail himself of the talents of others without wounding their feelings. This perhaps is the most useful quality which a man in a high public station can possess: since it is impossible that any mortal thus circumstanced can enter into all the details of business & perform every thing himself. He had too much magnanimity to feel jealousy, and he was too far removed from rivalship to be the cause of it in others. He did not prefer an opinion on account of its having originated with himself, nor was its value diminished in his estimation because it had originated with another. When the circumstances were not urgent, he was slow in deliberation, taking time to examine the question in every possible point of light. His mind was open to conviction so long as he was at liberty to suspend[150] his determination. But when the circumstances pressed, he was prompt & decisive. Yet sometimes, when the situation of affairs seemed to dictate the expediency of a provisional arrangement, he decided upon a partial but as he thought just view of the subject, and afterwards changed his decision, if he found sufficient motives to justify the change. For acting in this manner, his conduct appeared to be placed in a due medium between fickleness & obstinacy. He loved truth, he sought it unceasingly & he endeavoured to regulate all his actions by that standard.

The first conversation which General Washington ever held with any person on the question of his accepting or refusing the Office of the President of the United States (in case it should be offered to him; as, from the facts which gave rise to that conversation it appeared almost certain it would be) was with the Author of this work. The General had then resolved to decline accepting the Office, from a persuasion it was not necessary, as he believed that there were others better able than himself to perform the duties of it. After a conversation of four hours they seperated, the General receiving the counsel that it was proper to postpone his ultimate determination as long as the circumstances would allow without detriment to the public[151] cause. For several months afterwards they scarcely failed one day of conversing on the same subject or subjects connected with it. From a variety of considerations & correspondencies the General became convinced that it was his indispensable duty to accept the Presidency; and therefore made no hesitation in obeying the call of his Country when its choice was communicated to him by Congress thro' the organ of Mr. Charles Thompson.[152] In all this proceeding, which was then certainly unknown to the World, & which it has not been considered eligible should be published while he was living, there was nothing discoverable but the operation of reason without affec-

First in Peace (1866), engraving by John C. McRae. Courtesy of the Library of Congress. The painting depicts Washington's triumphal entry into New York as president on April 23, 1789.

tation. Influenced by principles of duty, his private inclination was overcome by a sense of public obligation.

The Person who is the subject of the preceding [biography] would have done honour to any age or nation in which he might have been born.[153] But he was perhaps more particularly calculated to be of singular utility in the times & circumstances in which he lived than in any other. He was formed to serve his country essentially by his example as well as by his actions. A few observations on his personal qualities, dispositions, & habits, which may claim indulgence for their veracity if not for their novelty, will conclude this note.

In pecuniary matters he was disinterested, but so far from[154] being negligent, that his private concerns were invariably arranged & managed with perfect regularity & oeconomy. He delighted much in seeing the pleasing results of the experiments & improvements which he had made in his farms. In the superintendence of which he was himself indefatigable. He was a pattern of neatness in every thing that belonged to him; and he was particularly fond of elegance united with simplicity in his dress, furniture & equipage. In his mode of living he was hospitable, without being ostentatious. In society he was always modest; & sometimes so reserved & so silent as to be accused of coldness or want of talents for conversation. With his friends (and it was generally his custom to remain at table in conversation with one or more of them for a considerable time after dinner) he was ever communicative, often animated & not unfrequently expressed himself with colloquial eloquence. No man probably ever appeared more different from himself as to the features of his face or in point of manners than he did at different times. Grave & majestic as he ordinarily was in his deportment, he occasionally, not only relished wit & humour in others, but displayed no inconsiderable share of them himself. He appreciated talents, but he distinguished between the splendid & the useful; and he held either the dearer to his heart from its being blended with honesty. It is[155] presumed that in his long & extensive intercourse with mankind, he paid a considerable attention to physiognomy in selecting persons for particular places; for in speaking of their various qualities he seldom failed (if they were not intimately known to him) to make some observations upon their exterior appearance. His moderation & firmness have been justly noticed amongst his distinguished characteristics. He ought not to be less advantageously known for his exemption from prejudices. On the other part the resources of his mind in useful ideas were copious & constant. His courage & prudence were equal to the exigencies of every crisis. Yet his attendants in the Army thought that he sometimes exposed his own person too much, especially in reconnoitring the enemy. In some instances, it would not have been difficult to have killed or taken him prisoner. But he deemed it very important to ascertain positions with his own eyes; and his attendants knew the value of his person better than he appeared to know it himself. When, in his dangerous sickness at New-York, soon after his election as President, & before the present Government was fully organised, he said to the Author: "I know it is very doubtful whether ever I shall rise from this bed, & God knows it is perfectly indifferent to me whether I do or not:" he was answered, "if, Sir, it is indifferent to you, it is far from being so to your friends and[156] your Country. For they believe it has still great need of your services." In proportion as his private as well as his public life shall be more known, a higher opinion will be entertained of his character. And nothing can more incontestably manifest the purity of his character in both than his confidential letters. His reputation as one of the principal persons engaged in founding the American Republic may safely be trusted to the page of history.[157]

Humphreys' Outlines
and Non-Biographical Material

Outlines for
"The Life of General Washington"

ROSENBACH MANUSCRIPT

1:37r

Introduction short & perspicuous (nearly as it now is) 2. (birth, genealogy, family) 3. Education, disposition, loss of father (brief on Virginian faulty education) 4. State of Society there (Williamsburg, Court in miniature) 5. his early introduction to company & public life.— 6. Encroachments & designs of the French to form a chain of Posts— 7. slightest & most energetic possible review of settlement & State of British Colonies in North America—Wars in consequence between European Powers— 8. Washington made one of the Deputy Adjutant Generals of Virginia—sent to warn the French to desist.— 9. His Journey & Report (clear, full, concise, narration).— 10. Troops first levied by Virginia—Colonel Fry, Lieutenant Colonel Washington—first campaign.— 11.— Braddocks campaign—Battle—best description I can give— 12. His plans, remarks on the wars in south—His journey to Eastward.—military matters untill the reduction of Fort

DuQuesne, resignation, marriage. Domestic & civil life untill the time of the Stamp Act. His property, industry, thrift. — Money passed through his hands. £6000 per Annum. cleared £3000 per Annum — Manner of living elegant & hospitable — extravagant fashion of drinking, in a manner absolutely necessary — his aversion, yet inevitable obligation to fall in with it. — [1]

YALE MANUSCRIPT

Folio 14

As David Humphreys is determined to write, for his own amusement & the information of posterity, the life of General Washington, in as clear, faithful & nervous a manner as he is able to do it; he solicits that General Washington will make a sufficiently large Common-place-book for minuting, at his leisure, such facts, informations, anecdotes of a military or private nature, portraits of characters, discriptions of battles, paintings of his own feelings, causes of his conduct as the General may think proper. It is of no importance tho loose & unconnected the observations are, nor need any attention be paid to the Chronological Order, if each event or remark, or anecdote, or character or description of action be kept seperate & by itself only noting the year — The Original Manuscript shall be either destroyed or restored to the General.

Notes on the following & many other points of similar nature will be interesting.

1. Any remarkable or characteristic facts of the family, his father's house burnt, his father's death, state of their affairs — his own education, Tutor, first years of life, personal strength, age, lively instincts in throwing stones — .

2. from the time he was to have gone on board a ship, untill his being appointed in the Adjutant General Department

(no matter how minute if the circumstances or events have any thing interesting or characteristic) going to West Indies—smallpox—his brother's death—

3. his first entrance on public life—going into company—interview with the Governor—the principles he laid down for his conduct, & acted upon.

4. Appointment to go to French Posts,—clear & strong, & [*illegible*]—detail of his Mission & report—

5. NB. Appointment in 1754 & actions of that Campaign are already described—That Affair has been represented in all the original French accounts as a most notorious violation of the laws of [*illegible*]—whether anything need be [*illegible*] articles of capitulation

6. The same is done with Braddock's campaign 1755 & the subsequent March of troops to Philadelphia—

7. Any one fact or more to mark the period in the campaigns of 1756 & 1757—

8. (Campaign of 1768 under General Forbes is described) but may be more particularly—farewell address & answer

9. Resignation—Marrying—going into domestic & farming life—

10. Regularity—system—manner of doing business—progressive wealth & dignity. as Member of Assembly, as a judge.[2]

Folio 15

[*Left column:*] private charities, benificence—Hospitality—& excess at home & abroad—(great reform & melioration of manners since)

———

At Williamsburgh a successive round of visiting & dinners it was not possible for a man to retire sober; without incurring imputations which even a person of philosophic cast did not choose to merit.—

———

State of the British empire at the close of the war—picturesque—

———

Stamp Act

———

measures alarming, part of the patriots—manufacturing—calm
& reasonable resistance—Virginia always took leading & dignified part—Colonel Washington's conduct—measures relaxed
—not relinquished. impolicy of continuing some trifling duties,
inflicting a wound & irritating it. The wound that had been
inflicted on the American government, often angered & never
healed, became incurable. courage. given by the bold eloquence
of a Chatham, the rapid sublimity of a Burk, the thunder-
ing mennaces of a Barre—the free spirit of investigation—
adventurous inquiries into the natural rights of man—political
writers who were read with approbation

Education (morals) indolence climate indulge & promote it

———

[*Right column:*] Locke &c—result of their theorems into short
political Creed that [*blank*]—Natural & artificial population,
progress of wealth & happiness, almost unparellelled—the state
of life favorable to independence of mind—equality in distribution of property & moderation in desires—Cities more
corrupt in morals & luxurious in habits, less capable of acting
with decision & making resistance than Country. Men of liberal professions spread every where & possessed of same sentiments—hence unanimity in appointing a Congress & simi-
larity in wording their Resolutions every soul breathed the
same [*blank*] & almost every voice pronounced the same alternative, of being prepared for freedom or death.— 1 *favorable*.
2 *unfavorable* circumstances of America for contending with
Britain.

———

When the tea ships were sent out, conduct in different Colonies, — nations not accustomed to nice discriminations in political disquisitions supposed were contending³ merely to be relieved from a duty of three pence per pound on the article of tea; instead of resisting the principle [*blank*] — which took our money without our consent. But the comprehensive words in the Declaratory Act were level to the lowest capacity & the British Parliament by asserting they had a right to make laws & bind [*illegible*] — saved from explanations — dissipation of youth — slavery &

———

Description of Williamsburgh, the manners & etiquette of a Court in miniature — Governor's Palace — Capitol — University — (Seat of Government convenient focus for business (merchants to meet & pleasure — birth right — ball; precedance; dress, imitation, [*illegible*]

———

nations in firing upon a flag of [*illegible*] — who commanded the attack at the Great Meadows? Was the [*illegible*]

———

Folio 18
1. His appointment Commander in Chief, hesitation to accept, motives — 2. progress to Boston, assumption of Command, state of confusion in which he found the army — wants — state of enemy — (objects that first struck his attention as necessary to be accomplished) system of reform adopted — of defence — of preparation for prosecuting the war another Campaign — distressing enemy for provision. 6. privateers fitted out — successful — Arnold ordered on secret expedition

———

In the mean time, view of operations South & plundering expeditions — Falmouth — New York, Rhode Island — operations in Virginia, Norfolk, Lord Dunmore — at the Southward — Indian

Agents — Captured at Sea — North Carolina — South Carolina — Georgia —

—————

Resume the Northern Affairs all in one series till death of Montgomery & Blockade of Quebeck

—————

Return in narrative to Boston & Cambridge untill evacuation

Folio 19

Hints — Heads &c — To make a commencement in middle 1. slight, but clear view of affairs before the first year of the war — 2. circumstances wrought up — 3. delusive expectations on the part of the British Parliament — 4. Conduct of the Congress of September 1774 — Hostilities — 5. Congress of May 1775 — 6. General Washington appointed, motives for it — no other person could combine the sentiments and affections of people in different parts of the Continent — His hesitation to accept — speech — 7. other appointments — officers that sat out with him from Philadelphia to Cambridge — occurrences & addresses — arrives & assumes command — 8. state he found the army in — confidence in him — no jealousy or rivalship — 9. his first objects of attention — enumeration of different branches of his charge — The character of the first & second army — Americans good subjects for soldiers — [4]

—————

Folio 21

The British ministry seemed to expect, that, if the Tea which was subject to that trifling yet obnoxious duty could be once landed in America, the bulk of the people would not have virtue enough to resist the inclination of using it.

—————

[*Left column:*] View of the situation of Great Britain at the Peace/and of America/alarm of the Stamp Act/conduct and firmness of the Colonists./relaxing & temporising policy of Britain retains dormant claims & trifling duties on certain articles, with the declaratory act/Misrepresentations — Ill offices done us by some Americans holding appointments/ Britain resumes the scheme of extracting substantial Revenue/ Not only leading men in the Colonies opposed — but the body of the people — no faction as pretended — [5]

———

[*Right column:*] A sketch of affairs public, without one word superfluous. — paint the circumstances that preceded & led on the Revolution so distinctly & concisely as to be equally entertaining & instructive, by arousing the attention & arresting all the faculties of the soul in contemplating the stupendous magnitude & wonderful progress of the Revolution, — which brought a world to political existence.

———

It will not be foreign from my main design to dilate somewhat largely on the circumstances

———

the causes & motives for the war Short.

Non-Biographical Material

[This section contains the material from Humphreys' notebooks that remains after the extraction of the text and outlines of the Washington biography. It includes historical reflections, letters, speeches — many written in Washington's voice — as well as other miscellaneous writings. All are reproduced, except for the lengthy book summaries of which Humphreys was so fond. Rather than include the entire summary of each book, I have simply cited the book in question. Although the authors and titles are usually apparent from Humphreys' summaries, it has not always been possible to determine the exact edition he read. In these cases, another contemporaneous edition has been cited.]

ROSENBACH MANUSCRIPT

1:1r

Dimidium facti, qui coepit, habet; Sapere aude. — Horace[6]

1:1r

Amount of Note due from Connecticut[;] send February 22 to Colonel Wadsworth

$$7\text{-}12\text{-}6$$

$$134\text{-} 6\text{-}6$$
$$134\text{-} 6\text{-}6$$
$$94\text{-}13\text{-}0$$
$$94\text{-}13\text{-}0$$

$$£457\text{-}19\text{-}0$$

1:27v, 28r, 28v

The following Address was transmitted from the Officers of the Virginia Regiment to Colonel Washington upon his resigning the command of it, in the close of the campaign 1758. —

To George Washington Esquire, Colonel of the Virginia Regiment, and Commander of all the Virginia Forces,

The humble Address of the Officers of the Virginia Regiment.

Sir.

We your most obedient & affectionate Officers, beg leave to express our great concern, at the disagreeable News we have received, of your determination to resign the command of that Corps, in which we have under you long served.

The happiness we have enjoyed & the honor we have acquired, together with the mutual regard that has always subsisted between you & your Officers, have implanted so sensible an affection in the minds of us all, that we cannot be silent on this critical occasion.

In our earliest infancy you took us under your tuition, trained us up in the practice of that discipline, which alone can constitute good troops, from the punctual observance of which you never suffered the least deviation.

Your steady adherence to impartial justice, your quick discernment and invariable regard to merit, wisely intended to inculcate those genuine sentiments of true honor & passion for glory from which the greatest military atcheivments have been derived, first heightened our natural emulation & our desire to excel. How much we improved by those regulations & your own example, with what alacrity we have hitherto discharged our duty, with what chearfulness we have encountered the severest toils, especially while under your particular directions, we submit to yourself; and flatter ourselves that we have in a great measure answered your expectations.

Judge, then, how sensibly we must be affected with the loss of such an excellent commander, such a sincere friend & so affable a companion. How rare is it to find those amiable qualifications blended together in one man? How great the loss of such a man? Adieu to that superiority, which the Enemy have granted us over other Troops; and which even the Regulars & Provincials have done us the honor publicly to acknowledge! Adieu to that strict discipline and order, which you have always maintained! Adieu to that happy union & harmony, which have been our principal cement!

It gives us an additional sorrow, when we reflect, to find our unhappy Country will receive a loss, no less irreparable, than our own. Where will it meet a Man so experie[n]ced in military Affairs? One so renowned for patriotism, courage, and conduct? Who has so great knowledge of the Enemy we have to deal with? Who so well acquainted with their situation & strength? Who so much respected by the soldiery? Who, in short, so able to support the military character of Virginia?

Your approved love to your King & Country, and your uncommon perseverance in promoting the honor & true interest of the Service, convince us that the most cogent reasons only could induce you to quit it: Yet we, with the greatest deference, presume to entreat you to suspend those thoughts for another year; and to lead us on to assist in compleating the glorious work of extirpating our Enemies, towards which so considerable advances have been already made. In you we place the most implicit confidence. Your presence only will cause a steady firmness & vigor to actuate in every breast; despising the greatest dangers, and thinking light of toils & hardships, while lead on by the Man we *know* and *love*.

But if we must be so unhappy as to part, if the exigencies of your affairs force you to abandon us; we beg it as our last Request that you will recommend some Person most capable to command; whose military knowledge, whose honor, whose conduct & whose disinterested principles we may depend upon.

Frankness, sincerity & a certain openness of soul are the true characteristics of an Officer; and we flatter ourselves that you do not think us capable of saying any thing, contrary to the purest dictates of our minds. Fully persuaded of this, we beg leave to assure you, that as you have hitherto been the actuating Soul of the whole Corps, we shall at all times pay the most invariable regard to your Will & pleasure; and will always be happy to demonstrate by our actions, with how much respect & esteem we are,

Sir. Your most affectionate & most obedient, humble servants

Fort Loudoun

December 31, 1758

	George Weedon	Robert Steward
	Henry Russell	John McNeall
	Jonathan Lawson	Thomas Woodward
	George Speak	Robert McKenzie
	William Woodford	Thomas Poullit
	John McCally	John Blagg
	John Pollard	Nathaniel Gist
James Craik Surgeon	W Hughs	Mordecai Bruckner
James Duncanson	Walt Cunningham	William Dangerfield
James Roy	William Cockie	William Fleming
	David Kennedy	Leonard Price
		Nathaniel Thompson
		Charles Smith

1:29r, 29v, 30r

ANSWER

To Captain Robert Steward and Gentlemen Officers of the Virginia Regiment.

My dear Gentlemen.

If I had words that could express the deep sense I entertain of your most obliging & affectionate address to me, I should endeavour to shew you that *gratitude* is not the smallest engredient of a character you have been pleased to celebrate; rather, give me leave to add, as the effect of your partiality & politeness, than of my deserving.

That I have for many years (under uncommon difficulties,

which few were thoroughly acquainted with) been able to conduct myself so much to your satisfaction, affords the greatest pleasure I am capable of feeling; as I almost despared of attaining that end — so hard a matter is it to please, when one is acting under disagreeable restraints! But your having, nevertheless, so fully, so affectionately & so publicly declared your approbation of my conduct, during my command of the Virginia Troops, I must esteem an honor that will constitute the greatest happiness of my life, and afford in my latest hours the most pleasing reflections.— I had nothing to boast, but a steady honesty— This I made the invariable rule of my actions; and I find my reward in it.

I am bound, Gentlemen, in honor, by inclination & by every affectionate tye, to promote the reputation & interest of a Corps I was once a member of: though the Fates have disjoined me from it now, I beseech you to command, with equal confidence & a greater degree of freedom than ever, my best services. Your Address is in the hands of the Governor, and will be presented by him to the Council. I hope (but cannot ascertain it) that matters may be settled agreeable to your wishes. On me, depend for my best endeavours to accomplish this end.

I should dwell longer on this subject, and be more particular in my answer, did your address lye before me. Permit me then to conclude with the following acknowledgments: first, that I always thought it, as it really was, the greatest honor of my life to command Gentlemen, who made me happy in their company & easy by their conduct: secondly, that had every thing contributed as fully as your obliging endeavours did to render me satisfied, I never should have been otherwise, or have had cause to know the pangs I have felt at parting with a Regiment, that has shared my toils, and experienced every hardship & danger, which I have encountered. But this brings on *reflections* that fill me with grief & I must strive to forget them; in thanking you, Gentlemen, with uncommon sincerity & true affection for the honor you have done me—for if I have acquired any reputation, it is from you I derive it. I thank you for also for the love & regard you have all along shewn me. It is in this, I am rewarded. It is herein, I glory. And lastly I must thank you for your kind wishes. To assure you, that I feel every generous return, of mutual regard—that I wish you every honor as a collective Body & every felicity in your private Characters, is, Gentlemen, I hope unnecessary—Shew me how I can demonstrate it, and you never shall find me otherwise than

Your most obedient,

New Kent County}

10th January 1759}

most obliged and

most affectionate

George Washington

1:34v, 35r

A List of the officers who were present, & of those killed and wounded in the action on the banks of the Monongahela the 9th day of July 1755.

STAFF

His Excellency Edward Braddock Esquire General & Commander in Chief of all His Majesty's forces in North America—died of his wounds—

Robert Orme Esquire} ———————————————— wounded

Roger Morris Esquire}—Aid-de-Camps ———————— wounded

George Washington Esquire} ————————————

William Shirley Esquire Secretary ———————— killed

Sir John St Clair Deputy

    Quartermaster General ———————————— wounded

Matthew Lesley Assistant to Ditto ———————— wounded

Francis Halket Esquire Major of Brigade ————————

44 REGIMENT

Sir Peter Halket Colonel ——————— killed
Lieutenant Colonel Gage ——————— slightly wounded
Captains Fulton ——————— killed
   Hobson ———————
   Beckwith ———————
   Getkins ——————— killed
Lieutenants Falconer ———————
   Littleler ——————— wounded
   Baley ———————
   Dunbar ——————— wounded
   Pottenger ———————
   Halket ——————— killed
   Freeby ——————— wounded
   Allen ——————— killed
   Simpson ——————— wounded
   Lock ——————— wounded
   Disney ——————— wounded
   Kennedy ——————— Ditto
   Townsend ——————— killed
   Preston ———————
   Nartlow ——————— Ditto
   Pennington ——————— wounded

48TH REGIMENT

Lieutenant Colonel Burton ——————— wounded
Major Sparks ——————— slightly Ditto
Captains Dobson ———————
   Cholmsley ——————— killed
   Bowyer ——————— wounded
   Ross ——————— wounded
Captain Lieutenant Morris ———————
Subalterns—Burbeck ——————— wounded

Waltsham ———————— Ditto
Crimble ———————— killed
Wideman ———————— Ditto
Hansard ———————— killed
Gladwin ———————— wounded
Hathorn ————————
Edmoston ———————— wounded
Cope ————————
Brereton ———————— killed
Hart ———————— Ditto
Montreseur ———————— wounded
Dunbar ————————
Harrison ————————
Cowhart ————————
W Mullen ———————— wounded
Crow ———————— Ditto
Sterling ———————— Ditto

ARTILLERY

Captain Orde ———————— slightly wounded
Lieutenants Buchannan ———————— wounded
McCloud ———————— Ditto
McCuller ———————— Ditto

ENGINEERS

Peter McKeller⎫
Robert Gordon⎬ Esquires ⎫ wounded.
Williamson⎭ ⎭

DETACHMENT OF SAILORS

Lieutenant Spinslove ———————— killed
Mr Haynes ———————— midshipman
Mr Talbot Midshipman ———————— killed
Captain Stone of General Lascelles
Regiment ———————— killed

Captain Floyer of General Warburton's ———— wounded

INDEPENDENT COMPANY OF NEW YORK.

Captain Gates ———————————————— wounded
Lieutenant Lumain ———————————— killed
Lieutenant Miller ————————————
Lieutenant Howarth of Captain Demerie's ——— wounded
Lieutenant Gray ———————————— Ditto

VIRGINIA TROOPS

Captain Stephens ———————————— wounded
Captain Wagoner ————————————
Captain Poulston ———————————— killed
Captain Paronie ———————————— Ditto
Captain Steward ————————————

VIRGINIA TROOPS

Subalterns — Hamilton ———————— killed
Woodward ————————————
Wright ———————————— killed
Splitdorff ———————————— killed
Stuart ———————————— wounded
Wagoner ———————————— killed
McNeale ————————————

According to the most exact return we can as yet get, about 600 men killed & wounded.

Taken from a return made by George Washington Esquire at the time.

D H———

26 Killed — 38 wounded, making 64 — out of 85 total in the action —

1:35v

Since the last Anniversary of Independence, My dear fellow Citizens, we have been witnesses to the complete establishment of a new general Government. On an event of such a magnitude, the voice of congratulation has already been heard from one extreme of our land to the other. But as our felicitations can never be more grateful than on the day,[7] that in which we are accustomed to commemorate the birth of our nation; so no occasion can be more suitable than the present, for employing our reflections on our political situation. I will therefore hope for your indulgence, while I make a few observations on the circumstances which attended the American Revolution; on the necessity which afterwards appeared for establishing a general government of more energy than the original Confederation; on the nature of the Government which has lately been carried into execution; and on the national prosperity which we may reasonably expect will result from the faithful administration of that Government.

––––––––

What then remains but for the several orders of men in Society to exert all the faculties which God hath conferred upon them, to accelerate this great & glorious event?[8] Thus circumstanced, we seem to want nothing to make us a happy people, but the persevering exertions of common sense & common honesty.

1:36r
But as our felicitations can never be more grateful than at the time when we are convened to commemorate the birth of our nation; it may perhaps be expected, from the task I am called upon to perform this day, that I shall be the organ for expressing the part you bear in this universal joy.[9] In the sincerity of our souls, we rejoice with our Countrymen in the happy prospect which now opens before us. But while we rejoice, we may remember, that no occasion can be more suitable than the present, for employing our reflections on our political situa-

tion. I feel a confidence, from the sensations of my own heart, that every bosom in this assembly beats high at the thought of our country's happiness. As the ardent eyes & the animated countenances, of all who compose it at this moment attest how sincerely they rejoice in the prospect before them. But while we rejoice, we may remember, that no occasion can be more suitable than the present, for employing our reflections, on our political situation.

1:37v

When a sympathetic disposition for the same objects silently prevails among such a great number of people, it requires only to be put in action properly directed. it requires not over-governing—securing liberty & protecting property—natural propensity in every person to better his condition.— To direct that effort

————

If any of the preceding observations, my dear fellow-citizens! are calculated to convince you, that the price of happiness is in your own hands, & that your political situation is far preferable to that of any other people, such observation, by tending to make you acquiesce in the divine goodness, will make you better citizens, better men, & better Christians.—

In a free country, every citizen is at liberty to offer his sentiments on all political subjects. I shall therefore claim the common previlege of mentioning some things, which I conceive would contribute eminently to promote the public good. Frugality & industry must be among the primary causes, that can render us happy & free.

————

As the distresses of individuals & the embarrassments of the Public have made men more frugal & more industrious, so I will candidly suppose that these very distresses & embarrassments will have been the remote, but real, cause of some portion of that prosperity, which will, perhaps, be wholly ascribed to the general Government.

1:38r

[*Summary of* Adam Smith, *An Inquiry into the Nature and Causes of the Wealth of Nations*, 3 vols. (Philadelphia: Thomas Dobson, 1787).]

1:38v

I accept the office of [*blank*], upon condition of being allowed to retire whensoever the circumstances will conveniently admit. This determination of acceptance is formed in consequence of the fullest consideration which I have been able to bestow on the subject; and you will permit me to add, not without a struggle which has occasioned uncommon distress.

Whatever might have been my desire of adhering to my resolution of remaining in retirement, I thought that the unanimous suffrages of a whole people ought to be preferred. Should this deference to the public sentiment be imputed to me by any one as a crime; I shall, however, have the satisfaction of not being reproached by my own conscience, for having acted from interested motives.

While, with an aching heart, I leave the enjoyments of private life, to encounter the fatigues, the troubles & not improbably the obloquy of public life; I carry with me the consolation that judgment of every individual on my conduct will at least be suspended, untill after I shall have had an opportunity of disclosing my reasons more fully to the two Houses of Congress.

In the mean time, penetrated with a due sense of this last & greatest token of affection & confidence which my Country could confer upon me; I promise that my endeavours shall be strenuously exerted to promote the welfare & glory of the United States.

I return my best thanks to both Congress, for the flattering manner in which they have communicated the choice that has fallen upon me; and to you, Gentlemen, for the urbanity with which you have executed their Commission.[10]

1:39r

The clouds, dark—roll'd from Heav'ns tremendous brow, Print their [*blank*] horrors on the wave below

1:39v

[*Summary of* Henry Swinburne, *Travels Through Spain, in the Years 1775 and 1776*, 2 vols., 2d ed. (London: P. Elmsly, 1787).]

1:40r

[*Summary continued of* Swinburne, *Travels Through Spain. Summary of* Henry Swinburne, *Travels in the Two Sicilies in the Years 1777, 1778, 1779, and 1780*, 2 vols., 2d ed. (London: P. Elmsly, 1783–85).]

1:40v, 41r

[*Summary continued of* Swinburne, *Travels in the Two Sicilies.*]

1:43v

[*Summary of* Philip Thicknesse, *A Year's Journey Through France, and Part of Spain*, 2 vols., 3d ed. (London: W. Brown, 1788).]

1:44r, 44v, 45r, 45v, 46r

[*Summary of* Maximilien de Bethune, duc de Sully, *Memoirs of Maximilien de Bethune, Duke of Sully, Prime Minister of Henry the Great*, 5 vols. (London: J. Rivington and Sons, 1778).]

1:46v

[*Summary of* Robert Watson, *The History of the Reign of Philip the Second, King of Spain*, 3 vols., 4th ed. (London: W. Strahan and T. Cadell, 1785). *Summary continued of* Sully, *Memoirs of the Duke of Sully*.]

1:47r

[*Summary continued of* Watson, *History of Philip the Second*.]

1:47v

[*Summary of* Thomas Clarkson, *An Essay on the Impolicy of the African Slave Trade* (Philadelphia: Francis Bailey, 1788). *Summary continued of* Watson, *History of Philip the Second*.]

1:48r

[*Summary of* William Coxe, *Travels into Poland, Russia, Sweden, and Denmark, Interspersed with Historical Relations and Political Inquiries*, 3 vols. (Dublin: S. Price, 1784).]

1:48v

Providence seemed disposed, in his early days, to try the temper of his courage by the most terrifying dangers & to prove the [*blank*] of his fortitude by the sharpest affliction.[11]

The unfortunate condition of the persons, whose labour in part I employed, has been the only unavoidable subject of regret. To make the Adults among them as easy & as comfortable in their circumstances as their actual state of ignorance & improvidence would admit; & to lay a foundation to prepare the rising generation for a destiny different from that in which they were born; afforded some satisfaction to my mind, & could not I hoped be displeasing to the justice of the Creator. —

"In order to regulate the assessments constitutionally, it will be necessary to take early measures for ascertaining exactly the number of Inhabitants in each of the States"

Loose page, side A
can be found to constitute [*blank*]

———

I cannot help flattering myself that the new Congress, for the self-created respectability & various talents of the members of which it must be composed, will not be inferior to any Assembly in the world. Insomuch I re[c]all—I can undertake to say little or nothing new, in consequence of the repetition of your opinion on the exp[e]diency there will be in accepting the office to which you refer. Your sentiments indeed coincide much nearer with those of my other friends, than with my feelings.

Greater & more substantial improvements are making it—manufactures, than were ever before known in America. In Pensylvania they have attended particularly to the fabrication of cotton-cloths, hose, hats, all articles in leather & many other articles. In Massachusetts they are instituting several extensive & useful branches. The number of shoes made in one town & nails in another is incredible. In that State & Connecticut are factories of superfine broad & other Cloaths.

I have been writing this day to our friend General Knox to procure me of the Hartford fabricated broad-cloath the pattern of a suit of Cloaths for my self. I think it will not be a great while before it will be unfashionable for gentlemen to appear dressed in any cloths, but those manufactured in the country. Population, you need not fear, will be progressive, so long as there shall be so many easy means of obtaining subsistance, & so ample a field for exertion of talents and industry.

I use no Porter or Cheese in my family, but such as is made in America—both those articles may be purchased of an excellent quality.

While you in Europe are quarelling among yourselves: while one king is running [*manuscript torn and illegible*]

Loose page, side B
so long as there shall continue to be so many easy means of obtaining a subsistence, & so long as there shall be so ample a field for the exertion of talents & industry.

Memoir in a new Government. On Instituting a Cabinet of Improvements, viz., a certain great Desk or Bureau. In our political existence as a government we have advantages superior to those possessed by any other nation in the world. We can wait ourselves.

To profit by the errors of other nations by avoiding the ill consequences which would result from similiar practices, is certainly the part of wisdom: to be careful not to entail impolitic systems of our invention, that of patriotism. As the plans now adopted may probably remain in practice for ages to come, & as it is much easier to prevent than remedy evils, we cannot be too solicitous to begin well. [*Blank*] Perhaps no better expedient can be devised for inducing every individual concerned in the Administration to act in a disinterested manner, than a knowledge that his actions will be laid open for the full investigation of all mankind. For this purpose, as well as for the purpose of concentering much useful information in one point, I would propose whether a Cabinet of Improvements ought not to be established, from the moment the new general Government shall be carried into effect. A Scheme of this kind has never been completely effected, though something like it was once proposed by the Duke of Sully & approved by Henry the Great.[12]

The Cabinet to consist of as many distinct Bureau's or Drawers, as there shall be different kinds of papers to be deposited in it. From each Head of a department, as soon as possible after his first entrance upon office under the general Government, a memoir should be obtained stating concisely & perspicuously the exact state of his Department at the time, when the new government begins to operate—for example, some the distinct [*manuscript torn and illegible*] If this project should be adopted, the papers deposited in the Cabinet would serve to justify the conduct of every honest man, whenever he should leave the Office of President, as well as for the Instruction of his Successors.

2:3r
State of the frontiers & causes of war—

YALE MANUSCRIPT

Folio 9
That some of the opponents to the proposed government have not laid aside their ideas of obtaining great & essential changes, by a *Constitutional opposition* (as they termed it) may be collected from their public speeches. That others will use more secret & perhaps insidious means to prevent it's organization may be presumed from their previous conduct on the subject. I have [*blank*]

It is reported that a respectable neighbour of mine has said; the Constitution cannot be carried into effect without great amendments. But I will freely do those on the opposite side the justice to declare, that I have heard of no cabals or canvassings amongst us. It is said to be otherwise with you.

Folios 10, 11

I flatter myself with the hope that the impediments which prevented your visiting America will be soon removed, & that we shall have the pleasure of witnessing to you personally our veneration of the Patriots of other Countries. In the interim, Mrs Washington requests that I will not omit to blend her best respects with mine for Lady Newenham & yourself.— It is with uncommon satisfaction that I seize on every occasion to assure

with how great truth & devotion
I have the honour to be

I failed not, on the receipt of your letter, to make the best arrangements in my power for obtain[ing] the oppossums & birds you mention. But I shall not be able to succeed in time for this conveyance. Having heard of a male & female oppossum, with several young ones at the house of one of my friends in Maryland, I sent for them — but unfortunately, they were all dead. I may probably be more successful before the Autumn.[13]

It is only necessary to add for your satisfaction, that, as all the States, which have hitherto assembled their Conventions & which are ten in number, have adopted the proposed Constitution, And as the concurrence of the States, would be sufficient to carry it into effect, in the first instance, it is expected the new Government will be fully organised & put in execution before the beginning of the ensuing year.

Folio 12

In a country so extensive and so partially known, it was natural that the boundaries between the Colonies of England & France should have been but imperfectly defined. The last Treaty between those Powers[14] had left the question still more vague & [*blank*]

Folio 13
& indeterminate.

The European Powers considered themselves as hav[in]g acquired a valid[15] title to lands in America by encompassing an Island, coasting a continent & especially by setting foot on the shore. While Vacant territory was so unbounded, there seemed to be little danger that interfering claims would produce a national contest.

Folio 17
The resolves of Towns & destricts[16] against persons who presumed to violate the recommendations of Congress operated in the nature of civil excommunications & excluded the delinquents from all the benefits of Society[.] There were instances where those who had been the most respected in their Villages, having thus forfeited the esteem of their neighbours, could neither procure mechanics or labourers to perform the ordinary offices which man owes to man in a State. They could hire no man to shoe a Horse, grind their corn, or assist in gathering their harvest. They wanted not the coat of tar & feathers, which was an American punishment sometimes inflicted on informers, & other worthless characters, for the censure of the People stigmatized them with a brand of infamy & sequestered them from the enjoyment of every social privilege. In this suspension of the forms of law & powers of government, it is

wonderful that less licentiousness should have prevailed than could have been expected at almost any other period.[17]

Folio 37

REMARKS

The seperate apartment should have locks and keys. The papers should be Numbered, & registered, so that, however numerous they might be [*illegible*] to, in a moment. A room in the Presidents house should be appropriated for this Cabinet, & should as a kind of Museum be stored with such models, plans, maps &c as may be deemed useful.

This Cabinet, if the proposal should be adopted, will shew the state in which every President found the Commonwealth at his entrance into office & in the State in which he left it—This Cabinet will therefore serve to place the character of every President, who acted openly & disinterestedly, in a favorable point of light, in spite of all the malice of Detraction; as well as to instruct his Successors in office, respecting the System of measures which had been follow[ed.]

As any tolerable System is infinitely preferable to the seemliness of improvident Parts and as the plans now to be adopted may probably remain in practice for ages, & as it is much easier to prevent than to remedy evils, we cannot be too solicitous to begin well. Happily for us, in commencing our political existence as a nation, we have advantages superior to those possessed by any other nation in the world. We can avail ourselves of the whole stock of experience, which mankind have hitherto acquired. Our task is improvement, rather than reformation. For we have fallen upon these latter days, when, as an infant nation we have few abuses to correct, & when, as an enlightened one, we may profit by the errors of older nations by avoiding the ill consequences which have resulted from the same ill practices. We want nothing to enable us to do well but common sense & common honesty aided by firmness & perseverance.

Folio 43

At the same time, I would wish it to be understood, as my opinion, that Candidates who may come forward recommending themselves to Offices with indecent boldness, or who through their friends shall make use of similar importunaty, would betray much greater signs of general merit & proofs of worthiness for a particular office, by being more modest or, at least less forward & less troublesome.

---

reasons why the design in forming the Constitution could not have been a conspiracy against the rights of America.

If I have any one[18] reason to fear that this government will not be carried happily into effect, or will not be productive of desirable prosperity; I will, not conceal my apprehension, that the danger will arise from locality. but as for warning on the sincerity of my soul, say that the ingracious Influence of locality should make the Authors of the national Councils postpone the general good, to the inferior consideration of what may be, in their judgment, profitable or popular, in particular district of the Union. My baneful apprehension that we may be Brokup on this rock, is founded on some experience of the selfishness of human nature; my great hope, that this tremendous consequence[19] will not ensue, on a knowledge of the disinterested patriotism of many of the characters[20] I have now the honour to address & the conviction of their Constituents that Union is the only refuge from ruin. In my public Administration, I have heretofore endeavoured invariably to shew that I gave no preferrence to one place over another. If contests & jealousies should appear (which Heaven forbid ever be), if example &

admonition in that case should not have no influence (though I would not too lightly or rashly despair of the Republic) I should begin to dread [*blank*]. But I will believe better things of you.

Folio 44
Let us expand our minds with the occasion—& extend our views with futurity.— Let us not be the politicians of the present point of duration, or the patriots of that single spot in which our Destiny happened to place us. United America, trembling, demands dispassionate deliberations, & magnanimous resolutions.[21]

America, comprised within the Union, has been a standing paradox, during her political existence: in war, her strength waxed mighty out of apparent weakness & her triumph astonished the doubtful Nations—in peace her impotence,[22] in the eyes of her friends, diminished the magnitude of her real resources & her inability to retaliate for insults excited the contempt of her enemies.

While the plough demands the first veneration, the forge is indispensable & the loom must not be neglected.

On the influx of foreigners—philosophic, patriotic, enthusiastic observations
    mathematics, chymistry, mechanics, architecture & [*blank*]

Let our conduct[23] with respect to foreigners who may choose to migrate to America be fairly understood that none who come may be scandalised or deceived. Talents which can be applied to the useful purposes of society, or lends art to mechanic rustic laborers, should be well received & may expect a decent support.[24] But those who expect to play the gentleman, or the knave: those who would wish to live by hereditary Titles or antirepublican idleness had better not come. We should desire to allure none by giving an artificial colouring to the natural advantages of the country.

No. 1

Appendix: The Pagination of the Yale Manuscript

THERE ARE forty-four loose pages of manuscript relating to David Humphreys' "Life of General Washington" in the Humphreys-Marvin-Olmsted Collection at Yale University. Because the pages are not numbered, and seem to be in no precise order, this chart provides a numbering scheme. In the left margin is the number I have assigned to the page; in the right, the first identifying words at the top left corner of each page.

Page	Identifying Words
1	The birth of GW [crossed out]
2	of dancing, fencing, riding
3	Though he was rather unsure & reserved
4	In these alarming circumstances
5	unelated with the [crossed out] of command
6	supported himself beneath the pressure
7	the throne, felt themselves
8	It would not comport
9	That some of the opponents
10	I flatter myself with the hope
11	erience of the States, would be sufficient
12	Sons: While heroes will [crossed out]
13	& indeterminate
14	As D. Humphreys is determined to write
15	private charities, benificence

Notes

Introduction

1. See, for example, Leon Howard, *The Connecticut Wits* (Chicago: University of Chicago Press, 1943), 243–45; John C. Fitzpatrick, ed., *The Writings of George Washington from the Original Manuscript Sources, 1745–1799*, 39 vols. (Washington, D.C.: U.S. Government Printing Office, 1931–44), 29:36.

2. John Pickering, ed., "The Braddock Campaign: From the Original Manuscript of Washington," *Essex Institute Historical Collections* 72 (1936): 89–101.

3. James Thomas Flexner, *George Washington and the New Nation (1783–1793)* (Boston: Little, Brown, 1969), 13n, and *George Washington: The Forge of Experience (1732–1775)* (Boston: Little, Brown, 1965), 355.

4. Edward M. Cifelli, *David Humphreys* (Boston: Twayne, 1982), 56. Other recent studies of Washington do not incorporate material from the Humphreys manuscript. See John Ferling, *The First of Men: A Life of George Washington* (Knoxville: University of Tennessee Press, 1988); Paul K. Longmore, *The Invention of George Washington* (Berkeley and Los Angeles: University of California Press, 1988); Barry Schwartz, *George Washington: The Making of an American Symbol* (London: Free Press, 1987).

5. Dumas Malone, ed., *The Dictionary of American Biography*, 22 vols. (New York: Charles Scribner's Sons, 1932), 9:373–75; Cifelli, *David Humphreys*, 15–19.

6. Cifelli, *David Humphreys*, 25–32; Howard, *The Connecticut Wits*, 122–23.

7. "Address to the Armies of the United States of America," in *The Miscellaneous Works of David Humphreys*, ed. William K. Bottorff (1804; reprint, Gainesville, Fla.: Scholars' Facsimiles and Reprints, 1968), 9, lines 85–86.

8. Howard, *The Connecticut Wits*, 122–23.

9. Emily Stone Whiteley, *Washington and His Aides-de-Camp* (New York: Macmillan, 1936), 5–8, 169, 188–207; Cifelli, *David Humphreys*, 32, 36, 45–47, 78; Douglas Southall Freeman, *George Washington: A Biography*, 7 vols. (New York: Charles Scribner's Sons, 1948–57), 6:277; *Dictionary of American Biography*, 9:373–75. For a discussion of Humphreys' version of Washington's inaugural address, see Flexner, *George Washington and the New Nation*, 162–68.

10. Freeman, *George Washington*, vol. 6, insert between pp. 63 and 64; Whiteley, *Washington and His Aides-de-Camp*, 188–92.

11. David Humphreys, "The Life of General Washington," 2 vols., AMs 1079/6, Rosenbach Museum and Library, Philadelphia, 1:3v (hereafter cited as Rosenbach MS).

12. Frank Landon Humphreys, *The Life and Times of David Humphreys*, 2 vols. (1917; reprint, St. Clair Shores, Mich.: Scholarly Press, 1971), 1:318.

13. Ibid.

14. Ibid., 1:320–21.

15. Ibid., 1:327.

16. Ibid., 1:330.

17. Quoted in Cifelli, *David Humphreys*, 54.

18. Humphreys, *Life and Times*, 1:358.

19. See, for example, Fitzpatrick, *Writings of Washington*, 30:2–4, 26–28, 125–29, 147, 165–66, 172–73, 287–88.

20. The other "Connecticut Wits" were John Trumbull, Timothy Dwight, and Joel Barlow. Howard, *The Connecticut Wits*, 180–81.

21. Donald Jackson and Dorothy Twohig, eds., *The Diaries of George Washington*, 6 vols. (Charlottesville: University Press of Virginia, 1976–79), 5:155; Freeman, *George Washington*, 6:85–87.

22. Humphreys, *Life and Times*, 1:424–26.

23. The exact date of Humphreys' arrival is unknown. In the Washington biography Humphreys says that he returned to Mount Vernon "in November." Washington first mentions Humphreys in his diaries on November 18, 1787. Humphreys-Marvin-Olmsted Collection, Box 4, Folder 151, Yale University Library, Manuscripts and Archives Division, 25 (hereafter cited as Yale MS); Jackson and Twohig, *Diaries of Washington*, 5:217.

24. Humphreys, *Life and Times*, 1:428–29; Cifelli, *David Humphreys*, 74–76; Howard, *The Connecticut Wits*, 246–47. At this time, Humphreys may have also begun a biography of Tench Tilghman, another of Washington's aides. The notes on this project are in the Humphreys-Marvin-Olmsted Collection, Yale University Library, Manuscripts and Archives Division, Box 4, Folder 152.

25. Jedidiah Morse, *The American Geography; or, A View of the Present Situation of the United States of America* (Elizabethtown, N.J.: Shepard Kollock, 1789), 127–32.

26. Rosenbach MS, 1:37r; Yale MS, 14, 18, 19.

27. Rosenbach MS, 1:2v.

28. Rosenbach MS, 2:1v.

29. Yale MS, 16.

30. Rosenbach MS, 2:15v; Morse, *The American Geography*, 132. Washington reiterated the point about foxhunting in a footnote in his "Remarks," *Forbes Magazine* Collection, New York, 11 (hereafter cited as Forbes MS). For Humphreys' later observations on Washington and foxhunting, see Yale MS, 25. For a further discussion of this topic, see the "Life of General Washington," n. 115, in this volume.

31. Direct quotes can be found in the Yale MS, 23, 24, 29, 30. At other times it is clear from the context that Humphreys is quoting, but there are either no quotation marks or incomplete quotation marks. See Yale MS, 22, 33, 35, 36.

32. Humphreys says the trip occurred in "the middle of July," but Washington's diary indicates that it occurred from May 30 to June 5, 1788. Yale MS, 28; Jackson and Twohig, *Diaries of Washington*, 5:334–36. For further discussion, see the "Life of General Washington," n. 125.

33. Freeman, *George Washington*, 6:157–66.

34. Pickering, "The Braddock Campaign," 89–90.

35. Forbes MS, cover page.

36. Pickering, "The Braddock Campaign," 89–90; Fitzpatrick, *Writings of Washington*, 29:50 n. 44. The precise descent went from Ann Bulkeley Humphreys to John Pickering to Henry Goddard Pickering to Sarah W. Pickering to the Pickering Foundation to John F. Fleming in 1974 to the Forbes Collection in 1988. See the auction catalogue published by Christie's, *Books and Manuscripts from the Estate of John F. Fleming*, auction held Friday, November 18, 1988, New York, 177.

37. See "The Guide to the Humphreys-Marvin-Olmsted Collection," and the "Lineage Chart of Families Represented in the Humphreys-Marvin-Olmsted Collection," Yale University Library, Manuscripts and Archives Division.

38. Pickering, "The Braddock Campaign," 90.

39. The transaction was dated February 13, 1935, voucher no. C4116. Letter from Leslie A. Morris to the author, December 14, 1988.

40. Forbes MS, 1.

41. Forbes MS, 1.

42. Forbes MS, 11, 1–10.

43. Compare Rosenbach MS, 2:2v and Yale MS, 3; Rosenbach MS, 2:8v and Yale MS, 8.

44. Rosenbach MS, loose page, side b; Yale MS, 37. These items are included in the Outlines and Non-Biographical Material in this volume.

45. Humphreys-Marvin-Olmsted Collection, Box 4, Folder 160, Yale University Library, Manuscripts and Archives Division, 5–12 (hereafter cited as Yale Copybook).

46. Morse, *The American Geography*, 127–32. For a partial list of the printings, see William S. Baker, ed., *Early Sketches of George Washington Reprinted with Biographical and Bibliographical Notes* (Philadelphia: J. B. Lippincott, 1904), 124–25. See also the Evans Early American Imprint Series, no. 22933 for the 1790 version and no. 27221 for the 1794 version. Neither Baker nor the Evans guide attributes the work to Humphreys.

47. Rosenbach MS, 2:2v–15v (verso sides only), 13r, 16r; Yale MS, 8; Forbes MS, 1–11.

48. Compare Yale MS, 8, and Morse, *The American Geography*, 129; Rosenbach MS, 2:15v, and Morse, *The American Geography*, 132; Rosenbach MS, 2:7v, and Morse, *The American Geography*, 128–29; and Rosenbach MS, 2:12v and Morse, *The American Geography*, 131. I would venture that pp. 1–8, 12–21, and 38–42 of the Yale MS form the draft version of vol. 2 of the Rosenbach manuscript, which in turn is published in Morse's *American Geography*.

49. Rosenbach MS, 2:4v; Morse, *The American Geography*, 128.

50. See Forbes MS, 1, and Morse, *The American Geography*, 127.

51. See Forbes MS, 11, and Morse, *The American Geography*, 129.

52. See the "Life of General Washington," nn. 19, 56, and 99, for these instances.

53. Rosenbach MS, 2:5v, 6v.

54. For the original draft, see the Forbes MS, 1–10. For the published version, see Morse, *The American Geography*, 128, which is also reprinted in the "Life of General Washington," n. 54.

55. Humphreys, *Life and Times*, 1:374.

56. Cifelli, *David Humphreys*, 54.

57. Yale MS, 14.

58. Quoted in William B. Sprague, *The Life of Jedidiah Morse, D.D.* (New York: Anson D. F. Randolf, 1874), 196.

59. Morse, *The American Geography*, vi.

60. Pickering, "The Braddock Campaign," 90–101; Fitzpatrick, *Writings of Washington*, 29:36–50, esp. 38 n. 43. Fitzpatrick's edition misdates Washington's "Remarks." The headnote lists it as having been written in October 1783. However, the document is contained in the volume for writings from 1786, suggesting that the 1783 date is a typographical error. Fitzpatrick, *Writings of Washington*, 29:36–50.

61. Bottorff, *Miscellaneous Works*, vi.

62. Howard, *The Connecticut Wits*, 241–70; Bottorff, *Miscellaneous Works*, vii–viii.

63. *Dictionary of American Biography*, 9:375.

64. Cifelli, *David Humphreys*, 8.

65. Humphreys, *Life and Times*, 2:313.

66. See Emory Elliott, *Revolutionary Writers: Literature and Authority in the New Republic, 1725–1810* (New York: Oxford University Press, 1982), 14.

67. David Humphreys, *An Essay on the Life of the Honorable Major-General Israel Putnam* (Hartford, Conn.: Hudson and Goodwin, 1788); John Fellows, *The Veil Removed from David Humphreys' "Life of Putnam"* (1843).

68. Humphreys, "Life of Putnam," in *Miscellaneous Works*, ed. Bottorff, 289.

69. Howard, *The Connecticut Wits*, 245. For other criticisms see Cifelli, *David Humphreys*, 74–76; Bottorff, *Miscellaneous Works*, x–xii.

70. The poems were "A Poem on the Death of General Washington," "Mount Vernon: An Ode," and Sonnet 12, "On Receiving the News of the Death of General Washington" in *Miscellaneous Works*, ed. Bottorff, 163–87, 223–25, 238.

71. Bottorff, *Miscellaneous Works*, 168, lines 177–82.

72. Rosenbach MS, 2:8v, 9v.

73. Humphreys, "Life of Putnam," in *Miscellaneous Works*, ed. Bottorff, 249.

74. Rosenbach MS, 1:4v. See also Rosenbach MS, 2:12v. For a further discussion of the role of history and biography in late eighteenth-century America, see Lester H. Cohen, *The Revolutionary Histories: Contemporary Narratives of the American Revolution* (Ithaca, N.Y.: Cornell University Press, 1980).

75. Yale MS, 8; Yale Copybook, 5.

76. Yale Copybook, 11.

77. See Humphreys' preface to his "Poem on the Love of Country," in *Miscellaneous Works*, ed. Bottorff, 121–23.

78. Cifelli, *David Humphreys*, 45, 78–79; Howard, *The Connecticut Wits*, 241; *Dictionary of American Biography*, 9:374.

79. Cifelli, *David Humphreys*, 95–96; Bottorff, *Miscellaneous Works*, 89–187.

80. Cifelli, *David Humphreys*, 101–2. If Humphreys had been more astute, his dismissal would not have come as such a surprise. The critic Leon Howard notes that "Jefferson, as secretary of state, had

found him a source of annoyance." Howard, *The Connecticut Wits*, 241–42.

81. Cifelli, *David Humphreys*, 118–20; Howard, *The Connecticut Wits*, 262–68; *Dictionary of American Biography*, 9:374–75.

82. Humphreys, *Life and Times*, 1:327; Cifelli, *David Humphreys*, 49.

83. Humphreys, *Life and Times*, 1:357.

84. Humphreys to Morse, May 17, 1806, Humphreys-Marvin-Olmsted Collection, Box 4, Folder 102, Yale University, Manuscripts and Archives Division.

85. Yale MS, 14. See also Rosenbach MS, 2:5v.

86. Forbes MS, 11.

87. W. W. Abbot, "An Uncommon Awareness of Self: The Papers of George Washington," *Prologue: Quarterly of the National Archives* 21 (Spring 1989): 7–19. Paul Longmore makes a similar point in *The Invention of George Washington*, esp. 52, 202–211.

88. Forbes MS, 7.

89. Forbes MS, 8.

90. Forbes MS, 4. After that time, Washington served in a voluntary capacity.

91. Forbes MS, 11.

92. Forbes MS, 3.

93. Forbes MS, 8.

94. Forbes MS, 7.

95. Forbes MS, 6.

96. Forbes MS, 7–8.

97. For a further discussion, see the "Life of General Washington," n. 40.

98. For a further discussion, see the "Life of General Washington," n. 52.

99. Forbes MS, 1.

100. Edmund S. Morgan, *The Genius of George Washington* (New York: W. W. Norton, 1980), 7; J. A. Carroll in *George Washington: Great Lives Observed*, ed. Morton Borden (Englewood Cliffs, N.J.: Prentice-Hall, 1969), 137; Freeman in *George Washington*, ed. Borden, 131. See also Marcus Cunliffe, *George Washington: Man and Monument*

(New York: New American Library, 1958), 149; Garry Wills, *Cincinnatus: George Washington and the Enlightenment* (New York: Doubleday, 1984), xix–xx.

101. Forbes MS, 6–7.

102. Forbes MS, 9.

103. Douglas Southall Freeman has stated that Washington found the experience so horrifying that he never wrote about it. W. W. Abbot acknowledges that Washington discussed the incident in the comments on Humphreys' biography, but he can find no other references to it. Freeman, *George Washington*, 2:358; W. W. Abbot, ed., *The Papers of George Washington*, Colonial Series, 6 vols. to date (Charlottesville: University Press of Virginia, 1983–), 6:122 n. 1.

104. See the account of Captain Thomas Bullitt in Abbot, *Papers of Washington*, 6:123.

105. Forbes MS, 8–9.

106. For contemporary accounts of the incident, see Abbot, *Papers of Washington*, 6:121–23 n. 1. For historians' accounts, see Freeman, *George Washington*, 2:357–58; Flexner, *Washington: Forge of Experience*, 216–17.

107. Forbes MS, 9.

108. Several recent works on Washington have also modified the traditional stereotype. See Ferling, *First of Men*; Schwartz, *George Washington*; and especially, Longmore, *The Invention of George Washington*.

109. Rosenbach MS, 2:12v.

110. Yale Copybook, 12.

111. Rosenbach MS, 2:10v.

112. Rosenbach MS, 2:2v; Yale MS, 1, 3. Flexner makes the point that the Humphreys manuscript is one of the few reliable sources of information about Washington's early education. Flexner, *Washington: Forge of Experience*, 24.

113. Yale MS, 40.

114. See the "Life of General Washington," n. 115.

115. Rosenbach MS, 2:14v.

116. Freeman, *George Washington*, 6:145–48.

117. Ibid., 6:141–66; Flexner, *Washington and the New Nation*, 153–60.

118. Harold C. Syrett, ed., *The Papers of Alexander Hamilton*, 27 vols. (New York: Columbia University Press, 1961–87), 5:222–23.

119. See, for example, Washington's letter of January 29, 1789, to the marquis de Lafayette. Fitzpatrick, *Writings of Washington*, 30:184–87.

120. Yale MS, 29.

121. Yale MS, 29.

122. For further information, see the "Life of General Washington," n. 131.

123. Yale Copybook, 8.

124. Yale Copybook, 8.

125. Yale MS, 31.

126. Yale Copybook, 8, 9. The first conversation about the presidency apparently occurred in June 1788, during the discussion about the impending arrival of the ship *Federalist*.

127. Yale MS, 35.

128. Yale MS, 35, 36.

129. Yale MS, 36.

130. Freeman, *George Washington*, 6:147–58; Flexner, *Washington and the New Nation*, 153–62. For Washington's responses, see Fitzpatrick, *Writings of Washington*, 30:109–12, 117–21, 141–43, 148–50, 184–87.

131. Yale MS, 23.

132. Howard, *The Connecticut Wits*, 245.

133. Mason L. Weems, *The Life of Washington* (1800), ed. Marcus Cunliffe (Cambridge, Mass.: Harvard University Press, 1962), 1–5; Rosenbach MS, 2:12v; Yale Copybook, 12.

Editorial Statement

1. On eclectic texts, see G. Thomas Tanselle, "The Editing of Historical Documents," *Studies in Bibliography* 31 (1978): 1–56.

2. David Humphreys, "The Life of General Washington," 2 vols., AMs 1079/6, Rosenbach Museum and Library, Philadelphia (Rosenbach MS).

3. Humphreys-Marvin-Olmsted Collection, Box 4, Folder 151, Yale University Library, Manuscripts and Archives Division (Yale MS).

4. George Washington, "Remarks," *Forbes Magazine* Collection, New York (Forbes MS).

5. Humphreys-Marvin-Olmsted Collection, Box 4, Folder 160 (Yale Copybook).

"The Life of General Washington"

1. Previous section from David Humphreys, "The Life of General Washington," 2 vols., AMs 1079/6, Rosenbach Museum and Library, Philadelphia, 1:1v (hereafter cited as Rosenbach MS). Alternate reading in Rosenbach MS, 1:2r: "If whole ages have sometimes elapsed without producing any thing worthy of rescuing them from oblivion; other ages have compensated for their barreness, by events uncommon in their nature, as interesting in their consequence. Such are &c."

2. Previous section from Rosenbach MS, 1:1v.

3. Previous section from Rosenbach MS, 1:2v.

4. Alternate reading: "facts."

5. Previous sentence inserted from Rosenbach MS, 1:3r, at Humphreys' direction.

6. Previous section from Rosenbach MS, 1:2v.

7. Previous section from Rosenbach MS, 1:3v.

8. Previous section from Rosenbach MS, 1:4v. Paragraph ends with: "for the concluding sentence," which seems to be a note from Humphreys to himself.

9. Washington's correct birth date was February 11, 1732, not 1734. Humphreys does provide the correct birth date elsewhere in the manuscript, at Rosenbach MS, 2:2v. Reform of the English calendar in 1752 pushed all dates forward by eleven days, giving us the cur-

rent date for Washington's birth. Douglas Southall Freeman, *George Washington: A Biography*, 7 vols. (New York: Charles Scribner's Sons, 1948–57), 1:47; James Thomas Flexner, *George Washington: The Forge of Experience* (Boston: Little, Brown, 1965), 12.

10. The Pope's Creek house, called Wakefield, was located about three-fourths of a mile from the Potomac River and about fifty miles from Richmond. Freeman, *George Washington*, 1:47 and cover lining; Flexner, *Washington: Forge of Experience*, 12 and cover lining.

11. Previous section from the Humphreys-Marvin-Olmsted Collection, Box 4, Folder 151, Yale University Library, Manuscripts and Archives Division, 16 (hereafter cited as Yale MS). An alternate reading of this passage is in the Rosenbach MS, 2:2v: "Notwithstanding it has often been asserted with confidence that General Washington was a native of some part of Great Britain, certain it is, his Ancestors came to this country from England so long ago as the year 1657. He, in the third descent after their migration to America, was born on the 11th. of February (Old Style) 1732, at the Parish of Washington, in the County of Westmoreland, in Virginia. The immediate family to which he belonged was numerous, & he was himself the first fruit of a second marriage. His education was principally conducted by a private Tutor." This was the opening used in the published version. See Jedidiah Morse, *The American Geography; or, A View of the Present Situation of the United States of America* (Elizabethtown, N.J.: Shepard Kollock, 1789), 127.

12. Previous section from Rosenbach MS, 2:3r.

13. Washington was the third, not the second, son of Augustine Washington, Sr. Augustine and his first wife, Jane Butler, had two sons who lived to adulthood, Lawrence and Augustine Jr. After Jane died, Augustine Sr. married Martha Ball. George was their first child. Freeman, *George Washington*, 1:41–47; Flexner, *Washington: Forge of Experience*, 11–16. Washington rectifies Humphreys' error in a note to the text. See George Washington, "Remarks," *Forbes Magazine* Collection, New York, 1 (hereafter cited as Forbes MS). Humphreys correctly identifies Washington as the first son of the second marriage in the Yale MS, 16.

14. Previous section from Yale MS, 1.

15. Previous section from Yale MS, 2. Alternate reading from Yale MS, 16: "In short, his juvenile years passed away, without being remarkable for any thing, but modesty, sedateness, & diligence."

16. Meaning "discrete," I believe.

17. Previous section from Yale MS, 3.

18. Previous section from Yale MS, 40.

19. Forbes MS, 1. Washington's father died on April 12, 1743, when George was eleven years old. Freeman, *George Washington*, 1:71–72; Flexner, *Washington: Forge of Experience*, 17. The published version in Morse's *American Geography*, 127, reads: "Previous to this transaction, when he was but ten years of age, his father died and the charge of the family devolved on his eldest brother."

20. Interlineation reads: "Capt. Gregory stationed in Virginia."

21. Previous section from Rosenbach MS, 2:2v. Alternate reading from Yale MS, 3: "His mother interposed with her intreaties & tears so irristably as to cause the project to be laid aside. Otherwise, instead of having led the armies of America to victory, it is not improbable he would have participated, as an Admiral of distinction in the naval triumphs of Britain."

According to Washington's biographers, in September 1746 (when George was fourteen, not fifteen, years old), Lawrence Washington sent one letter to George and one to his mother offering George the possibility of an appointment as a midshipman in the Royal Navy. After consulting family members, Mrs. Washington rejected the plan, partly because she did not want George to leave home and partly because she believed the Royal Navy did not offer George enough opportunities for advancement. It seems unlikely that the situation progressed to the stage where George's baggage was actually prepared for embarkation. Freeman, *George Washington*, 1:193–95; Flexner, *Washington: Forge of Experience*, 30–31.

22. Forbes MS, 1.

23. Forbes MS, 1.

24. Previous section from Rosenbach MS, 2:2v.

25. Previous section from Rosenbach MS, 2:2v.

26. After Lawrence Washington's death, Virginia was divided into

four (not three) districts. In each district, the adjutant was to instruct officers and soldiers in the use of arms and to discipline the militia. On November 6, 1752, George was appointed adjutant for the Southern District. The position, which paid one hundred pounds per year, was largely honorary and used as a route to preferment. Soon he received the more lucrative adjutancy of the Northern Neck, the position he really desired. Freeman, *George Washington*, 1:266–68; Flexner, *Washington: Forge of Experience*, 52–53.

27. Forbes MS, 1.

28. Previous section from Rosenbach MS, 2:3v.

29. Forbes MS, 1.

30. Previous section from Rosenbach MS, 2:3v.

31. Forbes MS, 1.

32. His trip lasted from October 31, 1753 to January 16, 1754. Donald Jackson and Dorothy Twohig, eds., *The Diaries of George Washington*, 6 vols. (Charlottesville: University Press of Virginia, 1976–79), 1:118–61. The publication he wrote was called *The Journal of Major George Washington, Sent by the Hon. Robert Dinwiddie, Esq.; His Majesty's Lieutenant-Governor, and Commander in Chief of Virginia, to the Commandant of the French Forces on Ohio. To Which Are Added, the Governors Letter, and a Translation of the French Officer's Answer* (Williamsburgh, Va.: William Hunter, 1754).

33. Previous section from Forbes MS, 1.

34. Previous section from Rosenbach MS, 2:4v.

35. Previous section from Rosenbach MS, 2:5v. Alternate reading from Rosenbach MS, 2:4r: "First Troops raised by Virginia] While England & France were still at peace in Europe, the Government of Virginia resolved to levy a body of troops for the defense of their frontiers. The object was to occupy the advantageous position, at the conflux of the Allegany & Monongahela, acording to the advice of Major Washington, before the French could establish themselves there in force. The command of the Virginia Levies was conferred upon Mr Fry, one of the Professors of the College, a person who was rendered inactive & unweildy, by reason of his age & corpulency; but who was supposed to be well acquainted with the theory of the mili-

tary art. Major Washington, whose zeal & capacity for business had already been displayed, was appointed his Lieutenant Colonel. But Colonel Fry soon died without joining the Corps, and the command devolved on Colonel Washington.

"Before this event took place, by the indefatigable industry of the Lieutenant Colonel & the other officers, who seconded his Measures, the Regiment was in great forwardness early in the Spring. Alexandria was the place of general rendevouz."

36. Previous section from Rosenbach MS, 2:5v.

37. Forbes MS, 1.

38. Forbes MS, 2.

39. Forbes MS, 3.

40. Washington's account here is notable for its glaring omission. The surrender document, written in French, stated that the Virginians were responsible for assassinating the French leader, Colon, sieur de Jumonville. Washington, who did not read French, claimed that his translator had rendered the word as "death" or "loss," not as "assassination." As a result, the surrender document generated widespread disapproval at home and abroad, since France and Britain were not officially at war. The historian James Flexner insists that the furor over the wording was actually a moot point, because "the preamble stated clearly that the English were being released because no state of war existed, and if no war existed, Jumonville had been wrongfully killed, whether or not Washington admitted that the Frenchman had been assassinated." Flexner, *Washington: Forge of Experience*, 104–6; Freeman, *George Washington*, 413–14.

41. Forbes MS, 4.

42. Forbes MS, 5.

43. Forbes MS, 6.

44. Forbes MS, 7.

45. Humphreys' insert from Forbes MS, 10.

46. For a list of those killed and wounded in this action, see Outlines and Non-Biographical Material, Rosenbach MS, 2:34v, 35r, in this volume.

47. Forbes MS, 7.

48. Forbes MS, 8.

49. Humphreys' insert from Forbes MS, 10.

50. Forbes MS, 8.

51. Douglas Southall Freeman was not aware that Washington ever wrote about this incident. W. W. Abbot concludes that Washington wrote about it only here, in the account for Humphreys. Freeman, *George Washington*, 2:358; W. W. Abbot, ed., *The Papers of George Washington*, Colonial Series, 6 vols. (Charlottesville: University Press of Virginia, 1983–), 3:122 n. 1.

52. Once again, Washington's account is notable for its omissions. Victory at Fort Duquesne, anticlimactic as it was, came despite, not because of, Washington. Forbes had rejected Washington's repeated (and sometimes impudent) suggestions that they travel to the fort using Braddock's road. Instead, a new, better road was cut and the French ultimately abandoned their refuge rather than fight. Flexner, *Washington: Forge of Experience*, 206–20; Freeman, *George Washington*, 2:322–35, 353–54.

53. Forbes MS, 9.

54. Paragraph compiled from Yale MS, 11. Washington first encamped at the Great Meadows on May 24, 1754. The attack by the French and Indians occurred on July 3, 1754. Jackson and Twohig, *Diaries of Washington*, 1:162–73; Freeman, *George Washington*, 1:403–5; Flexner, *Washington: Forge of Experience*, 101–4. There is an alternate reading of the paragraph in the Rosenbach MS, 2:5v, 6v: "The first action at which Colonel Washington was present, was on the [*blank*] of [*blank*] June [*blank*] at a place called the Great Meadows, where [*blank*]. In the next [*alternate reading:* "same"] summer he chose a position; above [*blank*] distant [*blank*], & erected a temporary work, which was called fort Necessity; here he was beseiged by [*blank*] & after [*blank*] days forced to capitulate, [*blank*] terms [*blank*], which the Savages violated."

The version in Morse's *American Geography*, 128, provides a fuller account of the incident: "Here he built a temporary stockade, merely to cover his stores; it was from its fate called fort *Necessity*. His force when joined by Captain M'Kay's regulars, did not amount to four hundred effectives. Upon receiving information from his scouts that a considerable party was approaching to reconnoitre his post, he rallied and defeated them. But in return he was attacked by an army, computed to have been fifteen hundred strong, and after a gallant defence, in which more than one third of his men were killed and wounded, was forced to capitulate. The garrison marched out with the honours of war, but were plundered by the Indians, in violation of the articles of capitulation. After this disaster, the remains of the Virginia regiment returned to Alexandria to be recruited and furnished with necessary supplies." This is the only substantial section in the published version that cannot be found in the original manuscript.

55. Previous section from Rosenbach MS, 2:6v.

56. The version in Morse's *American Geography*, 128, contains a slightly more illuminating version of this sentence: "Upon a royal arrangement of rank, by which 'no officer who did not *immediately* derive his commission from the king, could command one who did,' Colonel Washington relinquished his regiment and went as an extra aid de camp into the family of General Braddock."

57. Previous section from Rosenbach MS, 2:7v.

58. Previous section from Rosenbach MS, 2:8v.

59. Out of prudishness or delicacy, Humphreys seems to have mislabeled Washington's illness. See another reference to his "pulmonic disorder" in Humphreys-Marvin-Olmsted Collection, Box 4, Folder 160, Yale University Library, Manuscripts and Archives Division, 5 (hereafter cited as Yale Copybook). Throughout his early career, Washington was plagued by recurrent dysentery—what he himself calls, in one of his notes, "an inveterate disorder in his Bowels." Forbes MS, 9. For a list of Washington's illnesses from 1749 to 1769, see Bernhard Knollenberg, *George Washington: The Virginia Period, 1732–1775* (Durham, N.C.: Duke University Press, 1964), 119–20.

60. Previous section from Yale MS, 8. The next paragraph repeats the previous one in slightly different words: "His health was gradually re-established & Authentic documents are not wanting to shew the tender regret of which the Virginia line expressed at parting with their Commander, & the affectionate attachment he entertained

for them." A similar statement appears in Rosenbach MS, 2:8v: "In 1759, his constitution became very much impaired & many symptoms menaced him so seriously with a consumption, as to induce him to leave the service." For a copy of the "authentic documents" to which Humphreys refers, see Outlines and Non-Biographical Material, Rosenbach MS, 1:27v, 28r, 28v, 29r, 29v, 30r.

61. Previous section from Rosenbach MS, 2:8v.

62. Forbes MS, 11.

63. Alternate reading: "9000." According to Freeman, at its peak in 1797 Mount Vernon covered 8,251 acres. Washington held additional lands elsewhere. Freeman, *George Washington*, 6:392.

64. Previous section from Rosenbach MS, 2:9v. The manuscript continues from 2:9v to 2:10v, saying: "Soon after the war broke out, he was appointed by that Congress, Commander in Cheif of the forces of the United Colonies."

65. Previous sentence from Yale MS, 19.

66. Fragment placed before this sentence reads: "Shared in their triumphs & partook of their fame."

67. Paragraph compiled from Yale MS, 19, 20. An alternate reading from the same page says: "It required a course of years & a succession of provocations to dissolve those hopeful ties interwoven with our natures which seemed to be twisted in the fibres of our existence."

68. Paragraph compiled from Yale MS, 19, 20. Alternate reading compiled from Yale MS, 20: "Notwithstanding the little dreary intervals when the face of Britain was covered with a cloud & her arm shortened that it could not save, sunned by her eye & fostered by her hand[,] Our growth was like that of a vine, luxuriant, in its branches as prolific as in its fruits. But the arm of power would not wait for the vintage to fall as it matured into the lap of Britain. Though the grapes were green, orders were given for beginning to strip the Vine. Then it was seen, that gathered by premature avulsion & trodden in the wine-press of Ministerial wrath by mercenary Troops, the clusters produced blood instead of wine. Long had the mother country enjoyed the exclusive advantages of our commerce. We acquiesced &

were becoming daily more profitable to her. But seeing our flourishing state, she now assumed the right to levy indirect taxes."

69. Congress chose Washington as commander-in-chief on June
15, 1775. He made his reply on June 16, 1775. Worthington C. Ford,
ed., *Journals of the Continental Congress, 1774–1789,* 34 vols. (Washington, D.C.: U.S. Government Printing Office, 1904–37), 2:91–92.

70. Previous section from Yale MS, 4.

71. Interlineations: "with a noble diffidence"; "bespoke with a
noble disinterestedness."

72. Interlineation: "at the candour of." The speech continues:
"Tho' I am truly sensible of the high Honour done me, in this Appointment, yet I feel great distress, from a consciousness that my
abilities and military experience may not be equal to the extensive and
important Trust: However, as the Congress desire it, I will enter upon
the momentous duty, and exert every power I possess in their service,
and for support of the glorious cause. I beg they will accept my most
cordial thanks for this distinguished testimony of their approbation.

"But, lest some unlucky event should happen, unfavourable to my
reputation, I beg it may be remembered, by every Gentleman in the
room, that I, this day, declare with the utmost sincerity, I do not think
myself equal to the Command I am honored with.

"As to pay, Sir, I beg leave to assure the Congress, that, as no
pecuniary consideration could have tempted me to have accepted this
arduous employment, at the expence of my domestic ease and happiness, I do not wish to make any proffit from it. I will keep an exact
Account of my expences. Those, I doubt not, they will discharge, and
that is all I desire." Ford, *Journals of the Continental Congress,* 2:92.

73. Alternate reading: "upon."

74. Previous section from Yale MS, 5.

75. Previous section from Yale MS, 3.

76. Previous section from Yale MS, 3.

77. Previous section from Yale MS, 5.

78. Interlineation before this sentence reads: "disinterestedness."

79. Previous section from Yale MS, 6. Congress issued Washington's commission on June 17, 1775, and appointed four major generals

as his subordinates: Artemus Ward, Charles Lee, Philip Schuyler, and Israel Putnam. Horatio Gates was appointed adjutant general with the rank of brigadier general. Ford, *Journals of the Continental Congress*, 2:96–99.

80. Previous section from Yale MS, 6.

81. Washington's speech continues: "At the same time that with you I deplore the unhappy necessity of such an Appointment, as that with which I am now honoured, I cannot but feel sentiments of the highest gratitude for this affecting Instance of distinction and Regard.

"May your every wish be realized in the success of America, at this important and interesting Period; and be assured that the every exertion of my worthy Colleagues and myself will be equally extended to the re-establishment of Peace and Harmony between the Mother Country and the Colonies, as to the fatal, but necessary, operations of War. When we assumed the Soldier, we did not lay aside the Citizen; and we shall most sincerely rejoice with you in that happy hour when the establishment of American Liberty, upon the most firm and solid foundations, shall enable us to return to our Private Stations in the bosom of a free, peaceful and happy Country. I am etc." John C. Fitzpatrick, ed., *The Writings of George Washington from the Original Manuscript Sources, 1745–1799*, 39 vols. (Washington, D.C.: U.S. Government Printing Office, 1931–44), 3:305.

82. Previous section from Yale MS, 7.

83. Previous section from Yale MS, 38.

84. Previous phrase from Yale MS, 39.

85. This is undoubtedly a reference to what has come to be known as the Conway Cabal. During the winter of 1777–78, certain factions in Congress, especially the Massachusetts delegation, were increasingly hostile to Washington's handling of the war. At the same time, a group of military leaders, including Horatio Gates, Thomas Mifflin, and Thomas Conway, at least discussed the possibility of wresting control of the army from Washington. Washington discovered and exposed the plot, ending it without bloodshed. Freeman, *George Washington*, 3:586–605; Bernhard Knollenberg, *Washington and the Revolution: A Reappraisal* (New York: Macmillan, 1941), 65–77; John C.

Fitzpatrick, *George Washington Himself* (Indianapolis: Bobbs-Merrill, 1933), 333–51.

86. Previous section from Rosenbach MS, 2:10v.

87. Previous section from Rosenbach MS, 2:11v.

88. Previous section from Yale MS, 40.

89. Previous section from Yale MS, 41.

90. Previous section from Yale MS, 42.

91. Previous section from Rosenbach MS, 2:11v.

92. Previous section from Rosenbach MS, 2:12v.

93. Forbes MS, 11.

94. Previous section from Rosenbach MS, 2:13r.

95. Alternate reading: "On this account."

96. Previous section from Rosenbach MS, 1:36v. This was Humphreys' insertion from the same page, indicated by a "No. 1."

97. Previous section from Rosenbach MS, 2:12v.

98. Previous section from Rosenbach MS, 2:13v.

99. The version of this paragraph in Morse's *American Geography*, 131, adds a line: "It is then that every one present is called upon to give some absent friend as a toast; the name not unfrequently awakens a pleasing remembrance of past events, and gives a new turn to the animated colloquy."

100. Previous section from Rosenbach MS, 2:14v.

101. Humphreys' note from Rosenbach MS, 2:16r.

102. Previous section from Rosenbach MS, 2:15v.

103. Forbes MS, 11.

104. Forbes MS, 11. Location of Washington's note is my conjecture, as it is not marked in the text.

105. Forbes MS, 11. Location of Washington's note is my conjecture, as it is not marked in the text.

106. Note that neither Washington nor Humphreys mentions the fact that Washington owned slaves, even though he had 216 of them in 1786. Jackson and Twohig, *Diaries of Washington*, 4:277–83. For a comment on slavery written by Humphreys in Washington's voice, see Outlines and Non-Biographical Material, Rosenbach MS, 1:48v.

107. Previous section from Rosenbach MS, 2:15v.

108. Previous section is Humphreys' insert from Rosenbach MS, 2:16r.

109. Previous section from Rosenbach MS, 2:15v. The following sentence in the manuscript repeats an earlier statement: "To finish this account with the disclosure of an interesting fact, he manufactures linen & woolen cloths nearly or quite sufficient for the use of his numerous househould."

110. Previous section from Rosenbach MS, 2:1r.

111. Previous section from Rosenbach MS, 2:1v.

112. Previous section from Yale MS, 8.

113. Previous section from Rosenbach MS, 2:1v.

114. Alternate reading: "relish."

115. For much of his life, Washington had a passion for foxhunting. He took great care in breeding hounds and went to the hunt at least once every week in season. Humphreys mentions Washington's enthusiasm for the sport elsewhere in the manuscript, and Washington confirmed his interest in a note. See Rosenbach MS, 2:15v; Forbes MS, 11. After about 1788, however, his interest in the sport declined abruptly. By 1792 he no longer even owned hunting dogs. Humphreys' discussion in this part of the manuscript was obviously written at a later date than the earlier observations. See Fitzpatrick, *George Washington Himself*, 152; James Thomas Flexner, *George Washington and the New Nation* (Boston: Little, Brown, 1969), 27–28, 368–69.

116. The first mention of Humphreys' returning to Mount Vernon is in Washington's diary entry for November 18, 1787. Jackson and Twohig, *Diaries of Washington*, 5:217.

117. Previous section from Yale MS, 25.

118. Interlineation: "The recommendation of amendments should be [*illegible*]."

119. Alternate reading: "idea."

120. Previous section from Yale MS, 26.

121. Interlineation: "made a condition of ratification in the former."

122. It is true that Washington decided not to take part in the public debate over ratification, partly because of a lack of confidence in

his literary abilities and partly because he wanted to avoid suspicion that he was promoting himself for the presidency. Nevertheless, contrary to what Humphreys suggests, Washington was not reluctant to engage in private persuasion among those he knew and wrote numerous letters to friends and acquaintances urging adoption of the Constitution. He was indeed annoyed, however, when his private letters were published without his knowledge or consent. Fitzpatrick, *Writings of Washington*, 29:339–40, 380, 404; Freeman, *George Washington*, 6:129–30; Flexner, *Washington and the New Nation*, 141. For remarks on the ratification process written by Humphreys in Washington's voice, see Outlines and Non-Biographical Material, Yale MS, 9.

123. Calls for Washington to assume the presidency began almost as soon as the federal convention ended and continued until his actual election. Washington's letters to friends echo the ambivalent feelings about the presidency he expressed to Humphreys. See Freeman, *George Washington*, 6:145–50; Fitzpatrick, *Writings of Washington*, 30:65–67, 95–99, 109–12, 117–21, 148–50.

124. Previous section from Yale MS, 27.

125. Humphreys is mistaken about the date. According to Washington's diary, his trip lasted from May 31, 1788, to June 5, 1788. Washington was president of the Potomac Company, which planned to build a canal from the Great Falls in Virginia to Fort Cumberland, Maryland. He periodically attended meetings to assess the progress of the project, which was ultimately doomed to failure. He visited his brother Charles on June 3. Jackson and Twohig, *Diaries of Washington*, 5:334–36; Freeman, *George Washington*, 6:28–31; Flexner, *Washington and the New Nation*, 76–82.

126. On June 10, 1788, the Washingtons set out on an overnight trip to visit his sickly mother. Washington's relationship with his mother was apparently quite strained throughout his adult life, and he went to see her primarily out of duty rather than affection. Jackson and Twohig, *Diaries of Washington*, 5:339–40; Flexner, *Washington and the New Nation*, 36–38, 148, 173, 227–28.

127. Previous section from Yale MS, 28.

128. Alternate reading: "to this effect."

129. Previous section from Yale MS, 29. Interlineation: "& probably others in all instances would not."

130. Previous section from Yale MS, 30.

131. Washington noted the arrival of the ship in his diary entry for June 9, 1788. On July 24, 1788, the fifteen-foot ship, which was moored at the Mount Vernon wharf, sank in a violent storm. Jackson and Twohig, *Diaries of Washington*, 5:339, 366. Washington's "prudent" letter, dated June 8, 1788, and addressed to "William Smith and Others," read as follows: "Gentlemen: Captain Barney has just arrived here in the miniature ship called the Federalist; and has done me the honor to offer that beautiful *Curiosity* as a Present to me on your part. I pray you, Gentlemen, to accept the warmest expressions of my sensibility for this *specimen of American ingenuity:* in which the exactitude of the proportions, the neatness of the workmanship, and the elegance of the decorations (which make your Present fit to be preserved in a Cabinet of Curiosities) at the same time that they exhibit the skill and taste of the artists, demonstrate that Americans are not inferior to any people whatever in the use of mechanical instruments and the art of ship-building.

"The unanimity of the agricultural State of Maryland in general, as well of the commercial Town of Baltimore in particular, expressed in their recent decision on the subject of a general Government, will not (I persuade myself) be without its due efficacy on the minds of their neighbors, who, in many instances, are intimately connected not only by the nature of their produce, but by the ties of blood and the habits of life. Under these circumstances, I cannot entertain an idea, that the voice of the Convention of this State, which is now in session, will be dissonant from that of her nearly-allied sister, who is only separated by the Potomac.

"You will permit me, Gentlemen, to indulge my feelings in reiterating the heart-felt wish, that the happiness of this Country may equal the desires of its sincerest friends; and that the patriotic Town, of which you are Inhabitants (in the prosperity of which I have always found myself strongly interested) may not only continue to encrease in the same wonderful manner it has formerly done; but that its trade, manufactures and other resources of wealth may be placed permanently in a more flourishing situation than they have hitherto been. I am &c." Fitzpatrick, *Writings of Washington*, 29:516–17.

132. Previous section from Yale MS, 31.

133. Alternate reading: "might."

134. Previous section from Yale MS, 32.

135. Previous section from Yale MS, 33.

136. Robert Hanson Harrison was an Alexandria attorney and trusted friend of Washington. During the war, Harrison was one of his aides-de-camp; afterward, one of his favorite hunting companions. Harrison became chief justice of Maryland. Washington later nominated him for the U.S. Supreme Court, a position which he declined because of ill health. Harrison must have arrived June 10, 1788, while Washington was visiting his mother. Washington records that Harrison departed Mount Vernon on June 15. Jackson and Twohig, *Diaries of Washington*, 5:343; Emily Stone Whiteley, *Washington and His Aides-de-Camp* (New York: Macmillan, 1936), 13, 18, 27, 189–90, 202–3; Freeman, *George Washington*, 6:235, 238.

137. Alternate reading: "dialogue." Previous section from Yale MS, 34.

138. Previous section from Yale MS, 35.

139. Previous section from Yale MS, 36.

140. Previous section from Yale MS, 24. By the late fall Washington started to receive word of the outcome of the votes for the presidential electors, giving him a sure indication of his impending election. Fitzpatrick, *Writings of Washington*, 6:155–59; Flexner, *Washington and the New Nation*, 155–60.

141. Alternate reading: "must."

142. For a comment in Washington's voice on overeager candidates for appointment to office, see Outlines and Non-Biographical Material, Yale MS, 43.

143. Previous section from Yale MS, 22.

144. This is possibly a reference to John Adams, more probably to John Hancock. Both had been members of the troublesome Massachusetts delegation during the war. Nevertheless, the personal enmity between Hancock and Washington (dating back to Hancock's desire

to be named commander-in-chief) persisted, while Adams seemed to grow in Washington's favor. For example, the new president offered to share his carriage with Adams on a November 1789 journey from New York to Boston. In Boston, Governor Hancock gave Washington a studied insult, pleading sickness as an excuse not to pay the first call on the president. Washington returned the snub. (I thank Dorothy Twohig for this suggestion.) Freeman, *George Washington*, 6:154–57, 244–45; Flexner, *Washington and the New Nation*, 160–61.

145. Previous section from Yale MS, 23.

146. Previous section from Yale Copybook, 5.

147. Humphreys' note from Yale Copybook, 6.

148. Previous section from Yale Copybook, 6.

149. This is probably a reference to Washington's letter of July 25, 1785, in which he enthusiastically gave Humphreys permission to write his memoirs. Frank Landon Humphreys, *The Life and Times of David Humphreys*, 2 vols. (1917; reprint, St. Clair Shores, Mich.: Scholarly Press, 1971), 1:329–32.

150. Previous section from Yale Copybook, 7.

151. Previous section from Yale Copybook, 8.

152. For a draft by Humphreys of Washington's reply to Thompson, see Outlines and Non-Biographical Material, Rosenbach MS, 1:38v. For the actual reply, see Fitzpatrick, *Writings of Washington*, 30:285–86. As with Humphreys' inaugural address, Washington did not incorporate Humphreys' version into the final draft.

153. I have substituted the word "Biography" for "Poem." This section was originally written to follow Humphreys' presentation of his "Poem on the Death of General Washington," which was "Pronounced at the House of the American Legation, in Madrid, on the 4th Day of July, 1800; Being the Twenty-fourth Anniversary of the Independence of the United States of America." The poem, not including the epilogue, was first published in 1804. I have included the epilogue here as a conclusion to Humphreys' otherwise unfinished biography of Washington. William K. Bottorff, ed., *The Miscellaneous Works of David Humphreys* (1804; reprint, Gainesville, Fla.: Scholars' Facsimiles and Reprints, 1968), 149–87.

154. Previous section from Yale Copybook, 9.

155. Previous section from Yale Copybook, 10.

156. Previous section from Yale Copybook, 11. In mid-June 1789, less than two months after his inauguration, Washington developed a serious and perplexing illness, a persistent fever combined with a painful abscess on his left thigh. He recovered slowly, and only in early July did he begin to resume his presidential duties. Freeman, *George Washington*, 6:214–15.

157. Previous section from Yale Copybook, 12.

Humphreys' Outlines and Non-Biographical Material

OUTLINES

1. Periods added after numbers for consistency and readability.

2. Periods added after numbers for consistency and readability.

3. Interlineation: "it was a [*illegible*]."

4. Periods added after numbers for consistency and readability.

5. Slashes added to differentiate phrases on different lines of the manuscript.

NON-BIOGRAPHICAL MATERIAL

6. This is a quotation from Horace's *Epistles*, 1.2.40: "He who has begun has the half of it done; dare to be wise." Perhaps Humphreys was trying to encourage himself on the Washington project.

7. Alternate reading: "no day can be so dear to us that."

8. Alternate reading: "for the accomplishment of that end [*alternate reading:* "object"]?"

9. Interlineation: "with whic[h] pronounce."

10. This appears to be Humphreys' draft of Washington's reply to the formal announcement of his election to the presidency. The actual reply did not incorporate Humphreys' version. See John C. Fitzpatrick, ed., *The Writings of George Washington from the Origi-*

nal Manuscript Sources, 1745–1799, 39 vols. (Washington, D.C.: U.S. Government Printing Office, 1931–44), 30:285–86.

11. Alternate reading: "misfortune."

12. Humphreys' proposal regarding a cabinet is obviously based on his reading of Maximilien de Bethune, duc de Sully, *Memoirs of Maximilien de Bethune, Duke of Sully, Prime Minister of Henry the Great*, 5 vols. (London: J. Rivington & Sons, 1778). See Rosenbach MS, 1:44r, Loose page, side B, and Yale MS in the Outlines and Non-Biographical Material.

13. This section and the one above it are from Washington's letter of August 29, 1788, to Sir Edward Newenham. Fitzpatrick, *Writings of Washington*, 30:73–74.

14. Alternate reading: "Kingdoms."

15. Alternate reading: "good."

16. Meaning, I believe, "districts."

17. Alternate reading: "on common occasions."

18. Alternate reading: "I have but one."

19. Alternate reading: "misfortune."

20. Alternate reading: "characters, of many on whom I now turn my eye."

21. Alternate reading: "decisions."

22. Alternate reading: "impotent government."

23. Alternate reading: "ideas."

24. Alternate reading: "decently will such characters be supported."

Select Bibliography

Manuscripts

Humphreys, David. Copybook. Humphreys-Marvin-Olmsted Collection, Box 4, Folder 160, Yale University Library, Manuscripts and Archives Division.

——. "The Life of General Washington." Humphreys-Marvin-Olmsted Collection, Box 4, Folder 151, Yale University Library, Manuscripts and Archives Division.

——. "The Life of General Washington." 2 vols. AMs 1079/6, Rosenbach Museum and Library, Philadelphia.

Washington, George. "Remarks." *Forbes Magazine* Collection, New York.

Published Primary Sources

Abbot, W. W., ed. *The Papers of George Washington.* Colonial Series. 6 vols. to date. Charlottesville: University Press of Virginia, 1983–.

Baker, William S., ed. *Early Sketches of George Washington Reprinted with Biographical and Bibliographical Notes.* Philadelphia: J. B. Lippincott, 1904.

Bottorff, William K., ed. *The Miscellaneous Works of David Humphreys.* 1804. Reprint. Gainesville, Fla.: Scholars' Facsimiles and Reprints, 1968.

Fitzpatrick, John C., ed. *The Writings of George Washington from the*

Original Manuscript Sources, 1745–1799. 39 vols. Washington, D.C.: U.S. Government Printing Office, 1931–44.

Ford, Worthington C., ed. *Journals of the Continental Congress, 1774–1789.* 34 vols. Washington: U.S. Government Printing Office, 1904–37.

Humphreys, David. *An Essay on the Life of the Honorable Major-General Israel Putnam.* Hartford, Conn.: Hudson and Goodwin, 1788.

Jackson, Donald, and Dorothy Twohig, eds. *The Diaries of George Washington.* 6 vols. Charlottesville: University Press of Virginia, 1976–79.

Morse, Jedidiah. *The American Geography; or, A View of the Present Situation of the United States of America.* Elizabethtown, N.J.: Shepard Kollock, 1789.

Pickering, John, ed. "The Braddock Campaign: From the Original Manuscript of Washington." *Essex Institute Historical Collections* 72 (1936): 89–101.

Syrett, Harold C., ed. *The Papers of Alexander Hamilton.* 27 vols. New York: Columbia University Press, 1961–87.

Washington, George. *The Journal of Major George Washington, Sent by the Hon. Robert Dinwiddie, Esq.; His Majesty's Lieutenant-Governor, and Commander in Chief of Virginia, to the Commandant of the French Forces on Ohio.* Williamsburgh, Va.: William Hunter, 1754.

Weems, Mason L. *The Life of Washington.* 1800. Edited by Marcus Cunliffe. Cambridge, Mass.: Harvard University Press, 1962.

Secondary Sources

Abbot, W. W. "An Uncommon Awareness of Self: The Papers of George Washington." *Prologue: Quarterly of the National Archives* 21 (Spring 1989): 7–19.

Borden, Morton, ed. *George Washington: Great Lives Observed.* Englewood Cliffs, N.J.: Prentice-Hall, 1969.

Cifelli, Edward M. *David Humphreys.* Boston: Twayne, 1982.

Cohen, Lester H. *The Revolutionary Histories: Contemporary Narratives of the American Revolution.* Ithaca, N.Y.: Cornell University Press, 1980.

Cunliffe, Marcus. *George Washington: Man and Monument.* New York: New American Library, 1958.

Elliott, Emory. *Revolutionary Writers: Literature and Authority in the New Republic, 1725–1810.* New York: Oxford University Press, 1982.

Fellows, John. *The Veil Removed from David Humphreys' "Life of Putnam."* 1843.

Ferling, John. *The First of Men: A Life of George Washington.* Knoxville: University of Tennessee Press, 1988.

Fitzpatrick, John C. *George Washington Himself.* Indianapolis: Bobbs-Merrill, 1933.

Flexner, James Thomas. *George Washington and the New Nation (1783–1793).* Boston: Little, Brown, 1969.

——. *George Washington: The Forge of Experience (1732–1775).* Boston: Little, Brown, 1965.

Freeman, Douglas Southall. *George Washington: A Biography.* 7 vols. New York: Charles Scribner's Sons, 1948–57.

Howard, Leon. *The Connecticut Wits.* Chicago: University of Chicago Press, 1943.

Humphreys, Frank Landon. *The Life and Times of David Humphreys.* 2 vols. 1917. Reprint. St. Clair Shores, Mich.: Scholarly Press, 1971.

Knollenberg, Bernhard. *George Washington: The Virginia Period, 1732–1775.* Durham, N.C.: Duke University Press, 1964.

——. *Washington and the Revolution: A Reappraisal.* New York: Macmillan, 1941.

Longmore, Paul K. *The Invention of George Washington.* Berkeley and Los Angeles: University of California Press, 1988.

Morgan, Edmund S. *The Genius of George Washington.* New York: W. W. Norton, 1980.

Schwartz, Barry. *George Washington: The Making of an American Symbol.* London: Free Press, 1987.

Sprague, William B. *The Life of Jedidiah Morse, D.D.* New York: Anson D. F. Randolf, 1874.

Whiteley, Emily Stone. *Washington and His Aides-de-Camp.* New York: Macmillan, 1936.

Wills, Garry. *Cincinnatus: George Washington and the Enlightenment.* New York: Doubleday, 1984.

Index

Abbot, W. W., xxxviii, 105 (n. 51)

Adams, John, 114 (n. 144)

"Address to the Armies, An," xvi

Adjutancy of the militia, 8, 102 (n. 26)

Agriculture. *See* Farming

Aides-de-camp: of Washington, xvi–xvii

Alexandria (Va.), 11, 12, 13, 39, 41, 105 (n. 54)

Algiers, xxxvi

Allegheny River. *See* Fort Duquesne

American Geography, The: Humphreys' biography of Washington published in, xxi, xxvii–xxxi; comparison of, with Humphreys' manuscript, xxvii–xxix

American Revolution, xiv, xvi–xvii, 3, 53, 61–64, 74, 83–84, 86; Washington's participation in, 26–33

"Anarchiad, The," xx

Antifederalists, 41, 43, 48, 81–82

Baltimore, 44, 45, 113 (n. 131)

Barney, Captain, 44, 113 (n. 131)

Belknap, Jeremy, xxx

Bethune, Maximilien de, 77, 117 (n. 12). *See also* Cabinet

Biographies: of Washington, xiii, l–li; literary conventions of, xxxv, 96 (n. 74)

Braddock, Edward, xxxviii, xl–xli, 10, 58; ambush of, xlii, 15–18, 23; arrival in colonies, 14, 23; death and burial of, 19, 23

Bulkeley, Ann Frances. *See* Humphreys, Ann Frances Bulkeley

Burton, Ralph, 16, 71

Cabinet, 80–81, 84–85. *See also* Bethune, Maximilien de

Canada, 9, 29

Candidates for public office: Washington's attitude toward, 50–51, 85

Cartagena, xxviii, 8

Caunotaucarius, 10